NO WOMEN WITH FLAWS

BUSTING ALL MYTHS AND MAINTAIN TRANQUILITY OF WOMEN

SHAH SHABEENA SHOWKAT

Made with ❤ on the Notion Press Platform
www.notionpress.com

This book is dedicated to my parents and my family members....

"Sumaira ♡
Showkat Ahmad
Prince tariq
Zubair showkat
Faisal ahmad
Arsalan shah"

Contents

About Author

Shah Shabeena Showkat is born in Bandipora kashmir which is known as (Alim adab & aab) .she received her degree B.A through degree college of Bandipora and now currently she is pursuing her post graduation degree MA. ENGLISH in university of kashmir apart from that she wants to become an civil service officer to Responsible for improvement of social infrastructure and Curbing corruption to counter poverty...

About Book

The Book No Women With Flaws will give you a greater insight that Empowering women is to give women the right to express their views, educate them, to make them self-dependent and financially independent. We know that there always comes a moment in everyone's life when all they need is a spark of motivation. So this book can help you see a different perspective about women in Islam and guide you to owning your life and being the best you can be.

Introduction

In Islam there is absolutely no difference between men and women as far as their relationship to Allah is concerned, as both are promised the same reward for good conduct and the same punishment for evil conduct. The Qur'an says:

And for women are rights over men similar to those of men over women. (2:226)

The Qur'an, in addressing the believers, often uses the expression,'believing men and women' to emphasize the equality of men and women in regard to their respective duties, rights, virtues and merits. It says:

> "*For Muslim men and women, for believing men and women, for devout men and women, for true men and women, for men and women who are patient and constant, for men and women who humble themselves, for men and women who give in charity, for men and women who fast, for men and women who guard their chastity, and for men and women who engage much in Allah's praise, for them has Allah prepared forgiveness and great reward. (33:35)* "

This clearly contradicts the assertion of the Christian Fathers that women do not possess souls and that they will exist as sexless beings in the next life. The Qur'an says that women have souls in exactly the same way as men and will enter Paradise if they do good :

Enter into Paradise, you and your wives, with delight. (43:70)

Who so does that which is right, and believes, whether

male or female, him or her will We quicken to happy life. (16:97)

The Qur'an admonishes those men who oppress or ill-treat women:

> "*O you who believe! You are forbidden to inherit women against their will. Nor should you treat them with harshness, that you may take away part of the dowry you have given them - except when they have become guilty of open lewdness. On the contrary live with them on a footing of kindness and equity. If you take a dislike to them, it may be that you dislike something and Allah will bring about through it a great deal of good. (4:19)*"

Qur'an calls her muhsana - a fortress against Satan because a good woman, by marrying a man, helps him keep to the path of rectitude in his life. It is for this reason that marriage was considered by the Prophet Muhammad (peace be upon him) as a most virtuous act. He said: "When a man marries, he has completed one half of his religion." He enjoined matrimony on Muslims by saying: "Marriage is part of my way and whoever keeps away from my way is not from me (i.e. is not my follower)." The Qur'an has given the reason in the following words:
And among His signs is this, that He has created for you mates from among yourselves, that you may dwell in tranquillity with them; and He has put love and mercy between you. Verily in that are signs for those who reflect. (30:21)

The Prophet Muhammad (peace be upon him) was full of praise for virtuous and chaste women. He said:

"The world and all things in the world are precious but the most precious thing in the world is a virtuous woman. He once told the future khalif, ‘Umar: "Shall I not inform you about the best treasure a man can hoard? It is a virtuous wife who pleases him whenever he looks towards her, and who guards herself when he is absent from her."

On other occasions the Prophet said:

"The best property a man can have is a remembering tongue (about Allah), a grateful heart and a believing wife who helps him in his faith." And again: "The world, the whole of it, is a commodity and the best of the commodities of the world is a virtuous wife."

Before the advent of Islam women were often treated worse than animals. The Prophet wanted to put a stop to all cruelties to women. He preached kindness towards them. He told the Muslims: "Fear Allah in respect of women." And: "The best of you are they who behave best to their wives." And: "A Muslim must not hate his wife, and if he be displeased with one bad quality in her, let him be pleased with one that is good." And:"The more civil and kind a Muslim is to his wife, the more perfect in faith he is."

The Prophet (peace be upon him) was most emphatic in enjoining upon Muslims to be kind to their women when he delivered his famous khutba on the Mount of Mercy at Arafat in the presence of one hundred and twenty-four thousand of his Companions who had gathered there for the Hajj al-Wada (Farewell Pilgrimage). In it he ordered those present, and through them all those Muslims who were to come later, to be respectful and kind towards women. He said:

"Fear Allah regarding women. Verily you have married them with the trust of Allah, and made their bodies lawful with the word of Allah. You have got (rights) over them, and they have got (rights) over you in respect of their food and clothing according to your means."

In Islam a woman is a completely independent personality. She can make any contract or bequest in her own name. She is entitled to inherit in her position as mother, as wife, as sister and as daughter. She has perfect liberty to choose her husband. The pagan society of pre-Islamic Arabia had an irrational prejudice against their female children whom they used to bury alive. The Messenger of Allah (peace be upon him) was totally opposed to this practice. He showed them that supporting their female children would act as a screen for them against the fire of Hell:

It is narrated by the Prophet's wife, 'A'isha, that a woman entered her house with two of her daughters. She asked for charity but 'A'isha could not find anything except a date, which was given to her. The woman divided it between her two daughters and did not eat any herself. Then she got up and left. When the Prophet (peace be upon him) came to the house, 'A'isha told him about what had happened and he declared that when the woman was brought to account (on the Day of Judgment) about her two daughters they would act as a screen for her from the fires of Hell.

The worst calamity for a woman is when her husband passes away and, as a widow, the responsibility of maintaining the children falls upon her. In the Eastern World, where a woman does not always go out to earn her living, the problems of widowhood are indescribable. The Prophet Muhammad (peace be upon him) upheld the cause of widows. Most of his wives were widows. In an age when widows were rarely permitted to remarry, the Prophet encouraged his followers to marry them. He was always ready to help widows and exhorted his followers to do the same. Abu Hurairah reported that the Prophet said: "One who makes efforts (to help) the widow or a poor person is like a mujahid (warrior) in the path of Allah, or like one who stands up for prayers in the night and fasts in the day.

Woman as mother commands great respect in Islam. The Noble Qur'an speaks of the rights of the mother in a number of verses. It enjoins Muslims to show respect to their mothers and serve them well even if they are still unbelievers. The Prophet states emphatically that the rights of the mother are paramount. Abu Hurairah reported that a man came to the Messenger of Allah (peace be upon him) and asked: "O Messenger of Allah, who is the person who has the greatest right on me with regards to kindness and attention?" He replied, "Your mother." "Then who?" He replied, "Your mother." "Then who?" He replied, "Your mother." "Then who?" He replied, "Your father."

In another tradition, the Prophet advised a believer not to join the war against the Quraish in defense of Islam, but to look after his mother, saying that his service to his mother would be a cause of his salvation. Mu'awiyah, the son of Jahimah, reported that Jahimah came to the Prophet (peace be upon him) and said, " Messenger of Allah! I want to join the fighting (in the path of Allah) and I have come to seek your advice." He said, "Then remain in your mother's service, because Paradise is under her feet."

The Prophet's followers accepted his teachings and brought about a revolution in their social attitude towards women. They no longer considered women as a mere chattels, but as an integral part of society. For the first time women were given the right to have a share in inheritance. In the new social climate, women rediscovered themselves and became highly active members of society rendering useful service during the wars which the pagan Arabs forced on the emerging Muslim umma. They carried provisions for the soldiers, nursed them, and even fought alongside them if it was necessary. It became a common sight to see women helping their husbands in the fields, carrying on trade and business independently, and going out of their homes to satisfy their needs.

'A'isha reported that Saudah bint Zam'ah went out one night. 'Umar saw her and recognized her and said, "By God, O Saudah, why do you not hide yourself from us?" She went back to the Prophet (peace be upon him) and told him about it while he was having supper in her room, and he said, "It is permitted by Allah for you to go out for your needs." The predominant idea in the teachings of Islam with regard to men and women is that a husband and wife should be full-fledged partners in making their home a happy and prosperous place, that they should be loyal and faithful to one another, and genuinely interested in each other's welfare and the welfare of their children. A woman is expected to exercise a humanizing influence over her husband and to soften the sternness inherent in his nature. A man is enjoined to educate the women in his care so that they cultivate the qualities in which they, by their very nature, excel.

These aspects were much emphasized by the Prophet (peace be upon him). He exhorted men to marry women of piety and women to be faithful to their husbands and kind to their children. He said:

Among my followers the best of men are those who are best to their wives, and the best of women are those who are best to their husbands. To each of such women is set down a reward equivalent to the reward of a thousand martyrs.

Among my followers, again, the best of women are those who assist their husbands in their work, and love them dearly for everything, save what is a transgression of Allah's laws."

Once Mu'awiyah asked the Prophet (peace be upon him), "What are the rights that a wife has over her husband?" The Prophet replied, " Feed her when you take your food, give her clothes to wear when you wear clothes, refrain from giving her a slap on the face or abusing her, and do not separate from your wife, except within the house." Once a woman came to the Prophet with a complaint against her husband. He told her: "There is no woman who removes something to replace it in its proper place, with a view to tidying her husband's house, but that Allah sets it down as a virtue for her. Nor is there a man who walks with his wife hand-in-hand, but that Allah sets it down as a virtue for him; and if he puts his arm round her shoulder in love, his virtue is increased tenfold." Once he was heard praising the women of the tribe of Quraish, "...because they are the kindest to their children while they are infants and because they keep a careful watch over the belongings of their husbands."

The Shari'ah regards women as the spiritual and intellectual equals of men. The main distinction it makes between them is in the physical realm based on the equitable principle of fair division of labor. It allots the more strenuous work to the man and makes him responsible for the maintenance of the family. It allots the work of managing the home and the upbringing and training of children to the woman, work which has the greatest importance in the task of building a healthy and prosperous society.

It is a fact, however, that sound administration within the domestic field is impossible without a unified policy. For this reason the Shari'ah requires a man, as head of the family, to consult with his family and then to have the final say in decisions concerning it. In doing so he must not abuse his prerogative to cause any injury to his wife. Any transgression of this principle involves for him the risk of losing the favor of Allah, because his wife is not his subordinate but she is, to use the words of the Prophet (peace be upon him), 'the queen of her house', and this is the position a true believer is expected to give his wife. In contrast to these enlightened teachings of Islam in respect of women, Western talk of women's liberation or emancipation is actually a disguised form of exploitation of her body, deprivation of her honor, and degradation of her soul!

CHAPTER ONE

Five unknown and misunderstood issues about women in Islam

The issue of women's rights in Islam has been a contentious area of discussions and intense debates both in the Muslim world and in the West. The two dominant mainstream narratives have victimized Muslim women, though in different ways. On one hand, many Muslims and Muslim governments appropriate Islamic text to justify discrimination against women and to impose social and legal restrictions on women's rights and freedoms. On the other hand, Western islamophobic neo-orientalists use these popular yet traditional misogynistic readings of Islam to support their xenophobic claims against Islam and Muslims.

This leaves Muslim women in a dilemma. Muslim women who want to be good Muslims and want to also have their rights experience conflict and frustration under these popular interpretations. At the same time, they struggle to respond to Western attacks on Islam. These women (and men) react defensively that "Islam honors and protects women, and grants them full rights" but without having access to solid religious foundations and scholarship. Meanwhile, any attempts to discuss women's rights and freedoms in the Middle East are labeled imperialist colonialist western hegemonic enterprises that corrupt the piety of Islamic moral fabrics and traditions. Genuine attempts to protect Muslim women from discrimination through the international models of gender equality and empowerment programs end up alienating local contexts and will be likely unsuccessful without giving the local communities proactive and independent roles. Evidently, the issue of women in Islam is complex and multifaceted. What remains constant, though, is that Muslim women emerge as the victims in all these accounts.

In contrast to these mainstream narratives and the popular traditional interpretations of Islamic text, a solid (although still peripheral) feminist Islamic perspective has emerged. The less known narrative is that of Islamic jurisprudence female scholars who provide contextual readings and alternative interpretations of Islamic text. These Muslim women, who are also practicing believers, dispute the misogynistic Islamic interpretations that subordinate women in Muslim societies, and demonstrate -in the name of their faith- that the popular prejudiced readings of Islam are not inherent in the text but are products of their time and place.

The issue of women in Islam is very intricate and requires a great level of theological, linguistic and historic expertise and skills to understand and analyze. Below is but a brief introductory summary of these alternative readings, referencing some of the work of experts in Islamic jurisprudence and human rights scholarship, and my ensuing recommendations for advancing women's rights in the Middle East.

Five unknown and misunderstood issues about women in Islam

1. Patriarchal traditions colored the early and dominant interpretations of the Qur'an

The foundations of Islamic Law are based on the Qur'an. In addition, the Sunnah (the hadith and the example of the prophet) is used as a secondary source for further clarification and guidance. When the Qur'an and Sunnah leave an issue unresolved, Muslim scholars resort to ijtihad – the science of interpretations and rule making, where they can supplement Islamic Law with local customs. Naturally, scholars from different communities and schools of thought disagree in their ijtihad, which is unobjectionable as long as these scholarships are based on religious and linguistic knowledge and are conducted piously and in good faith. While Muslims are free to choose the interpretations most convincing to them, it is inevitable that these individual ijtihads are influenced by the patriarchal customs and beliefs of their surroundings.

According to Dr. Aziza al-Hibri, professor emerita of Law at the University of Richmond and one of the leading scholars in Islamic law and human rights; medieval Islamic jurisprudence and the dominant schools in ijtihad adopted today, are largely influenced by the patriarchal traditions of their times. These patriarchal cultural assumptions became deeply rooted in ijtihads and Islamic jurisprudence to the point that such patriarchal structures are inaccurately believed to come from the Qur'anic text itself. In addition, the free practice of ijtihad was restricted by authoritarian political establishments in order to preserve their political interests. As a result, the subsequent mainstream interpretations became based on authoritarian patriarchal interests and imposed by nation states.

> "
>
> *It is therefore evident that Muslim jurists are a product of their societies, where the central patriarchal concept that men are superior to women influenced understanding of Qur'anic texts. As such, these ijtihads are a product of their times and patriarchal circumstances, and need to be addressed and re-evaluated. In the words of Dr. Asma Lambrabet, a leading figure in revising Islamic texts from feminist perspectives; "Islamic thought should evolve in order to redefine and rethink itself, and to make the necessary distinction between the spiritual message and certain interpretations that have frozen the text, occasionally suffocating its true message."*
>
> "

2. Alternative non-patriarchal interpretations of the Qur'an do exist

As many Islamic scholars point out, the Qur'an clearly instates the principle of equality among all humans. In the Qur'an (Qur'an 49:13, among other verses), God created humans from male and female, and despite the empirical differences among humans (based on race, gender, etc.), the Qur'an regards them as equals and only ranks humans based on their moral choices and piety. God created men and women from the same soul, as guardians of each other in a relationship of cooperation not domination.

However, while some specific verses at face value seems to be promoting male dominance, alternative interpretations are important to consider. For example, one the most controversial and most commonly cited Qur'anic verse to justify male dominance is the 34th ayah in surat al-Nisa', which is most commonly interpreted as "men are the protectors and maintainers" (original: qawwamun, other possible interpretations: advisors, providers of guidance) "of women," "because" (original: bima, other possible interpretations: in circumstances where) "they are superior to them" (original: faddala, other possible interpretations: have a feature that the other lacks) "and because" (original: bima, other possible interpretations: in circumstances where) "they support them from their means."

The popular interpretation understood in light of patriarchal hierarchal traditions, as al-Hibri demonstrates, can be completely different once patriarchal assumptions are eliminated. In this case, the Qur'an was describing a specific situation observed at that time, where a man takes the responsibility of an advisory role if both these conditions are present; first if the man has an ability that a particular woman lacks, and second when the man is maintaining that particular woman, meanwhile the woman is free to reject the advice. Based on the rules of Islamic jurisprudence, when one verse is specific to certain circumstances, the more general principle of equality (outlined above) is to be taken as the general rule while the particular instance as the exception.

It is important to note herein that this is only one example and there are numerous other cases where the dominant patriarchal interpretations are disputed by feminist Islamic jurisprudence scholars. While family law and personal status codes in Arab and Muslim countries restrict women's rights and freedoms (e.g., in choosing a husband, guardianship/ wali, obeying the husband/ ta'ah, initiating divorce, dowry requirement, polygamy, marriage to non-Muslims, etc.), alternative interpretations of the Qur'an dispute these claims of male domination based on religious texts (see al-Hibri).

3. Context matters

The mainstream interpretations of Qur'anic text that consider men superior to women are therefore not objective but subjective human interpretations heavily influenced by historic and geopolitical conditions. In addition, Qur'anic verses in many instances are revealed in very specific circumstances, and need to be understood based on contextual terms.

For example, surat al-Baqara 282, is another of the commonly cited verses to claim male superiority in Islam. The verse, revealed in a business context, states that "when you enter a transaction involving a debt for a fixed period reduce it to writing and let a scribe write it down between you in fairness ... and bring two witnesses from among your men. Should there not be two men, then a man and two women of the women you choose to be witnesses." If taken out of context, this verse could be interpreted to suggest that a woman's testimony is not equal to that of a man's. However, considering the specific situation of a business transaction and the larger context in which women at the time were not involved or experts in business affairs, this verse should not be taken as evidence that women are not equal to men in Islam. In fact, in another instance, the second successor to the Prophet, Umar ibin Khattab, appointed a woman to manage the affairs of a market in Medina.

Therefore, verses of the Qur'an need to be taken in the contexts in which they were revealed, as the Qur'an takes the specific circumstances of the societal conditions into consideration.These specific verses are products of their times and contexts, and need not be forced onto different times and different contexts. Moreover, the Qur'anic verses need to be looked at in a wholesome manner and not taken in isolation from other texts and verses. In fact, the five main schools of thought in Islamic jurisprudence (Hanafi, Maliki, Shafi'i, Hanbali, and Ja'fari), formally adopted by Muslim countries, agree on four basic principles of Islamic law; it changes with time and place, must serve the public interest, should not cause harm, and may be discarded if its cause has faded.This is clear evidence that some verses which were revealed in specific circumstances should not be taken out of context and generalized as the rule for all times and places.

4. Muslim women's rights are attainable through Islam

According to Dr. al-Hibri, the Islamic philosophy of change embraces gradual change, and is linked to the principle of shura where societal affairs are conducted in consultation. The Islamic philosophy of change is also linked to the important Qur'anic principle of no compulsion in the matters of faith. Gradualism, shura, and aversion to coercion are important Islamic principles that are most appropriate to advance the rights of Muslim women. Gradual stable change to the status and rights of Muslim women is therefore achievable through Islam. Two of the agreed upon principles of Islamic law: rationality ('illah; when a reason for a law disappears, so must the law) and public interest (maslahah; Islamic laws must serve the public interests, including those of women) are important foundations for revising patriarchal laws and re-engaging in ijtihad. As such, Muslim women's rights can be attained through these Islamic jurisprudential principles and requirements.

5. Liberation must come from within the Islamic domain

As al-Hibri points out, Muslims women tend to be religious, and would not react well to a western feminist perspective that is imposed upon them, therefore secular approaches to women's rights are not likely to 'liberate' Muslim women because people of faith will continue to want to follow their perception of the Divine Will.

> ***" In addition, many scholars argue that there is no universal model of gender quality ('one size fits all'), and the West should not keep a monopoly on the topographies of modernity and truth.***
>
> ***In this context, liberation and change must come from within the Islamic sphere, where Muslim women have a proactive and autonomous role in reform, re-reading of the Qur'an, and revealing the historical prejudices that colored the understanding of the Qur'anic message. In an environment of religious devotion, liberation must be rooted in the roots of the Qur'an. "***

Recommendations for advancing women's rights in the Middle East

Today female Muslim scholars are making their voices heard through their re-readings of Islamic text, and their call for the Qur'anic approach in uprooting the patriarchal principles that are very difficult to change. This alternative reading of the Qur'an and the Islamic approach to change are essential components for achieving women's rights in the Middle East.

As many women and women's organizations in the Middle East and in the world, who are dedicated to eliminating discrimination against women, face great challenges by current Islamic laws and religious figures, it is vital for them to incorporate the above alternative interpretations of Qur'anic text into their work. Here are some specific recommendations to better promote women's rights and achieve gender equality in the Middle East.

- Because Islam is used against women, it is essential to engage with the religion in order to clarify misunderstandings and misconceptions among those who use the religion to oppress women. As most Muslim women seek to behave in accordance with the teachings of Islam, understanding the religion is important and liberating for Muslim women. The popularization of these alternative interpretations as well as alternative religious education in the Middle East can provide Muslim men and women the tools to advocate gender equality in Islam and through Islam. Gender equality programs need to incorporate an Islamic feminist component and religious education into all their projects, and support Muslim women in their efforts to re-engage with the Qur'anic

•While the alternative readings of the Qur'an are particularly important to popularize among men and women of faith and the Islamic approach to change is an essential element in achieving women's rights, these efforts need to be implemented within a broader approach. Culture is dynamic and contextual; it interacts with, influences and is influenced by religious and legal systems. Just as patriarchal traditions infiltrated interpretations of Islamic text, these dominant interpretations prevented the much needed changes to patriarchal traditions. In this case, these Islamic interpretations legitimized the patriarchal customs, where the conservative Islamic interpretations are often brought up against any attempt to reform laws or change patriarchal traditions. As such, a holistic multi-dimensional approach that incorporates all social, legal, and religious foundations of gender discrimination needs to be adopted.

• Interpretations are, after all, interpretations. While some may agree with the alternative non-patriarchal interpretations of Islamic text, others may continue to believe in and use the misogynistic prejudiced readings of Islam. Moreover, as al-Hibri herself points out, interpretations are subject to the influence and control of powerful entities and their interests. While the call for alternative re-readings of the Qur'an is certainly imperative, empowering, and liberating for Muslim women, national legal systems are likely to remain welcoming of the patriarchal Islamic readings, for various (and rather obvious) reasons. In addition, secular women living in Muslim countries do not have alternative legal systems under such frameworks, and therefore must abide by religious interpretations they might not agree with. As such, while these non-patriarchal Islamic interpretations are necessary for those who choose to act in accordance with their faith, non-religious legal systems must be made available for others.

•Based on the above point, a separation of religion and state and a legal system that grants women full rights and freedoms can be incorporated into the commanded change to the dominant patriarchal social and religious systems. While most Muslim scholars reject what they call the external imposition of the universal models of gender equality on Muslim societies, this dichotomous framing of external vs. internal is rather inaccurate and even misleading. These universal models of women's rights are based on basic principles of freedom and equality and many women and organizations in Muslim countries are heavily involved in these international efforts. The most recent international legislation regarding gender equality is the United Nations Convention on the Elimination of All Forms of Discrimination Against Women (CEDAW) adopted in 1979 and ratified by 189 states, which is comparable to a bill of human rights for women. All Arab countries have signed and ratified the Convention on the Elimination of All Forms of Discrimination Against Women (CEDAW) but with so many reservationsthat defeat the purpose of the convention. Meanwhile, Arab and Muslim countries continue to impose some the worst discriminatory daily practices against women in the world, with religious, social, and legal justifications. While religious reform and alternative interpretations are an essential part of the change process, international efforts and the progress they have achieved need not be overlooked.

As such, the gradual change to these multi-dimensional patriarchal systems must be a composite effort that incorporates feminist re-readings of the Qur'an, social and economic change, and legal reform based on the principles of CEDAW. Additionally, this holistic approach to advancing the rights and freedoms of women in the Middle East cannot work without giving the primary role to local voices. Finally, the ultimate goal need be the promotion and legalization of women's full rights as basic human rights.

CHAPTER TWO

A Womens Verginity is Between Her and God

Today, hundreds of Indonesian women are forced to have virginity tests done in order to join the police force.

Iraqi women face court ordered virginity tests after allegations from husbands that they are not virgins after the first day of marriage.

Women all across the globe are expected to bleed on their wedding nights as proof that they are pure.

If such a doubt is cast as it is in this day and age, the humiliation and shame that a woman is forced to feel is beyond reproach. Virginity has been a long misunderstood issue, and a source of shame or honor in the Muslim community. No one seems to want to talk about it until marriage age begins to creep up, when it is apparently permitted for a girl to go from not talking or interacting with any men to choosing the one to live with one for the rest of her life. The expectation that is placed upon a woman to remain "chaste" and pure for her husband is beyond that of any other, from her intelligence to her exemplary character. No one wants to talk about the tens of medals and awards a woman has achieved, her college career at an Ivy League, or the fact that she has taught herself how to speak four different languages — but everyone wants to discuss whether or not blood had been spilled on her wedding night.

BUT, WHAT IF THERE'S NO BLEEDING?

Many fail to realize that not all women bleed after they lose their virginity. The fear, however, is perpetuated by archaic rituals such as showing the blood on the sheets after the wedding night. In itself, this is a social construct put in place to make women feel bad about their sexuality and pass judgement on them. This is especially sensitive at the time of marriage when a woman may be publicly shamed and abused for not remaining a virgin for her wedding night. These disastrous consequences force many women to undergo hymen reattachment surgery in order to save their future honor — mostly for their family's honor. But even more troubling is the fact that only a woman's sexual past is publicly scrutinized. Islamically, we are asked to hide the sin of a fellow Muslim, not publicly shame them for it. However, this seems to only be subjected to one sex more than the other.

> “*"These disastrous consequences force women to undergo hymen reattachment surgery in order to save their future honor – mostly for their family's honor."*”

It may be in some cases that a woman has indeed lost her virginity previous to marriage. But as Muslims, we put our trust and faith in Allah (SWT) and know that the sins we have committed in the past are not a reflection of ourselves.

Rather, the realization of the sin and the actions taken toward forgiveness is what determines true character.

The most conservative interpretations of Islam understand premarital sex to be one of the deadliest sins a Muslim can commit, but even then, are we not taught Allah (SWT) is most forgiving? Here is where it becomes interesting, though. It is within the most conservative of communities that one may find the double standard, which is manifested to somehow forgive the man, but continue to shame the woman.

Here's something to think about: If we are such good people, shouldn't we be discreet about the acts of others since it is between them and Allah (SWT)? I mean, that is what we are taught.

In an ironic twist of fate, however, we seem to be living in communities that continue to refuse refuse forgiveness for one sex while making amends for another. Even most interesting is the expectancy of forgiveness by Allah (SWT) by those same judgmental individuals who are quick to ask you about your discrepancies.

Forget the fatwas that allow you to ask your spouse about their virginity. In fact, that practice should be discouraged altogether. The truth is that your relationship with your future spouse will be determined by character and values. Again, Islam tells us that we should not confess our sins to anyone but Allah (SWT). We know that we are not to disclose the wrong doings of others, including our own.

"To judge one's intention is to belittle him; and to belittle him is a form of pride; and to have an atoms worth of pride in your heart is enough to forbid you from entering paradise."

Abu Hurayrah (may Allah be pleased with him) said: I

heard the Messenger of Allah (sallallaahu ‘alayhe wa sallam) say:

> “
>
> *“All of my ummah will be excused, except for the Mujaahireen (those who make their sins known). And verily it is a kind of Mujaaharah (exposing one’s sins) that a man does something (sinful) at night, and then in the morning, when Allah has screened his sin for him, he says, ‘Hey So and-So! I did such-and- such last night...’ And the night passed with His Lord screening him, and he wakes up casting aside the screen of Allah from himself.”* ”

BUT THEY STILL ASK ABOUT YOUR VIRGINITY.

The case of virginity does not seem to be as important for men as it is for women. This is evident when suitors (and their parents) speak to a girl and her family. They ask her about her past and question her chastity (virginity).

Who are you to ask so publicly about something that does not concern you? And I say “does not concern you” because you are not asking me if I pray, or read Qur’an, or what kind of children I want to raise. Instead, you are asking me about something extremely inconsequential to the future of our relationship together.

Maybe more important (future in-laws) is to look upon your son and ask him the same questions you want to know about the girl. Chastity pertains to all prior to marriage, not just women. How innocent is the son you have raised? If you feel uncomfortable asking your son this question, why would you feel comfortable asking a woman? More importantly, where did your son get the idea that it was okay to ask that of a woman?

IS YOUR SON A VIRGIN?

Perhaps this question would be less revolting and given more importance if this was a degree that we used to judge both man and woman. But it is not.

If anything, the idea of virginity is just another form of control. From an Islamic perspective, yes, physical intimacy is an act that is sacred between husband and wife. But from the way this ruling it practiced culturally, almost no value is given to the religious importance. If there was, there would be more scrutiny on the sexual history of men in the community as well. So many of our communities have a "boys will be boys" attitude, but please someone tell me where in the Qur'an it says a woman's virginity weighs heavier than a man's virginity? Hint: it doesn't exist.

Muslim women have this expectation placed on them, that if they want to be "good girls" they have to remain virgins until they are married. Okay, cool. Your value as a woman is based on some weird social construct of innocence, but what does it say about the way we interpret religion when we only enforce practices on women? Well...then it slowly stops becoming religion.

> *"So many of our communities have a "boys will be boys" attitude, but please someone tell me where in the Quran it says a woman's virginity weighs heavier than a man's virginity?"*

We see this all the time in our communities: A Muslim man who has a questionable past, where it's known he has had multiple sexual partners, wants to get married. He makes a lists of demands, including that his future wife has "remained pure." The troubling part is that society lets him do that. Mothers believe that after this period of "experimentation," their sons will eventually fall right into place after marrying a so called "chaste" woman – that somehow this attribute in the woman will change him for the better. His past is his past, but a woman's past is her future.

> "
>
> *Perhaps we would think this was less cultural if the same invasive question was asked of the man, rather than it turning into some bizarre method of classifying women as "good girl" or "bad girl." Because really, what else is it?*"

CHAPTER THREE

Misconceptions and The Rights of Women in isLam

Allah (SWT) has created both men and women without subordination of one another. Islam has ensured gender equality and women's rights in every sphere of their life. Islam has guaranteed rights of men and women in an equal degree and there is no discrimination between men and women. But due to the prevailing socio-cultural norms and practices in Bangladesh sometimes the guarantee of Islam do not get translated into tangible actions. Islam is the religion which liberated Muslim women by ensuring equal rights to them in comparison to their male fellow. There are some misconceptions prevailing in Bangladesh regarding women's rights in Islam. Sometimes Muslim women themselves falsely knew that they are backward and oppressed by their religion. Some make great mistake in presuming that all conduct and practices of a Muslim are connected to Islam. The prime object of this study is to pick out how rights of women are ensured in Islam. This study concludes with an allusion that women are not subordinate of men and indicate an avenue to identify properly women in the light of Islam. This research is actually qualitative in nature where only secondary data has been used. Analytical method was also used in this research. Data has been collected from various books, journals, holy Qur'an and sunnah (tradition) of the Prophet (peace be upon him). This research finds that Islam does not deprive the women rather ensuring proper rights, dignity and status but due to lack of proper Islamic knowledge and awareness and sometimes to dominate or neglect some misconceptions prevailing in Bangladesh. To eliminate prevailing misconceptions regarding women rights in Islam proper Islamic knowledge and awareness of the women is essential. The core implication of this research is that it will play a vital role to eliminate prevailing misconceptions regarding women rights in Islam and to ensure the rights, dignity and status of women as given in Islam. This study will open a new avenue for scholars who will be able to contribute their knowledge and wisdom to ensure the position of women as given in Islam. This research includes only those rights of the women as guaranteed by Islam and it does not include constitutional rights or other rights ensured by the existing laws of the country.

Undoubtedly, there is no discrepancy in Islam between men and women as far as their relationship to Allah in concerning as both are promised the same reward for good conduct and the same punishment for evil conduct. Allah says:

> "
>
> *"And for **women are rights** over men similar to those of men over women." (2: 228)* "

The holy Quran, in addressing the believers, often uses the expression "believing men and women" to accentuate the equality of both male and female in regard to their particular duties, rights, virtues and merits. Islam is such a religion which has first given to the women a place of dignity and honour because before the advent of Islam, there were huge discriminations towards women. Islam abolished inhumanity, inequality, discrimination towards women as well as gave a complete code of conduct for both male and female. Prior to the arrival of Islam, the pagan Arabs used to bury their female children alive, make women dance naked in the vicinity of Ka'ba during their annual fairs and treated women just like slaves or chattels and they used women only for their sexual contentment who possess no rights, dignity, honour or position . Unlike other religions, which regarded women as being possessed of inherent sin and wickedness and men are being possessed of inherent virtue and nobility, Islam treats men and women as being of the equal essence created from one soul. Allah says:

> "
>
> ***"O mankind, be mindful of your duty to your Lord, who created you from a single soul and from it created its mate and from the two created and spread many men and women". (4: 2)***"

To understand the rights, honour, dignity and status of women in Islam, it is sufficient to judge the position of women before the advent of Islam. At that time, they were like slaves and most often their positions were worse than animals. The Prophet (peace be upon him) proposed to stop any sorts of torture, cruelty or inhuman to women. He showed greatness towards them. He advised the Muslims: "Fear Allah in respect of women." And: "The best of you are them who behave best to their wives." And: "A Muslim must not hate his wife, and if he is displeased with one bad quality in her, let him be pleased with one that is good." And: "The more civil and kind a Muslim is to his wife, the more perfect in faith he is" . The Prophet (peace be upon him) was very much forceful in enjoining upon Muslims so that they are kind to the women. In his Farewell Pilgrimage , he directed those present, and through them all those Muslim whoever to came later, to be courteous and kinds towards women. He said: "Fear Allah regarding women. Verily you have married them with the trust of Allah, and made their bodies lawful with the word of Allah. You have got (rights) over them, and they have got (rights) over you in respect of their food and clothing according to your means". In Islam spiritual equality have guaranteed for both men and women. Allah says, :

> "*"Whoso does good whatever male or female, and is a believer, shall enter Paradise and they shall not be wronged a whit." (4:125)*"

But currently in many Muslim communities women are not consider according to the rights given them in Islam. In many societies Muslim are practicing their own cultures and customs and women are being subject to cultural issues, patriarchal features of their society and also political oppression. In Bangladesh as majority of the people are Muslim, Islam plays a significant role in the country.

Although Quran and the tradition of the Prophet (peace be upon him) emphasis on gender equality and rights, dignity and status of women but somebody use it for exploiting and discriminating against women after tempering some verses of the text to dehumanize them .

In Bangladesh many misconceptions prevailing regarding women's rights due to proper religious knowledge, misinterpretation of Quran and the tradition of the Prophet (peace be upon him). The power to explain the religious rules is preserved by men in Bangladesh as women are not so qualified in religious knowledge and for this reason patriarchal importance is reflected and sometimes it is politicized as the Ulema (religious scholars) are mostly men. Due misconceptions and misinterpretations of Islamic rules women are being deprived of their rights, dignity, honour and status as given them in Islam and sometimes are being subject of oppression. To prevent domination of male, women's subordination and to ensure rights of women in Bangladesh as given in Islam by abolishing misconceptions about women's rights proper religious knowledge as well as awareness of women is essential.

Rights and Status of Women Prior to the Advent of Islam

In the pagan society of pre-Islamic Arabia the status of women was like slaves who had no rights and dignity. Women would not get share either from parents or spouse as inheritance. But Islam ensures share of women in the property of parents and husband Regular shape of marriage as we understand at present time was totally absent. There were such types of marriage as may be treated as fornication, prostitution, adultery or polyandry. Men could marry any number as he like and there were no specific rules in regard to marriage, they could marry even two real sisters at one and at the same time . But in case of marriage, Islam imposes prohibition on account of affinity (prohibition due to marriage relationship). In this respect the Holy Qur'an declares:

"Forbidden for you (to marry) are the mothers of your wives and your step-daughters that are in your laps (in charge of you) through your wives to whom you have gone in; but if you have not gone in to them, then there is no sin upon you (to marry them); and the wives of your sons whom you have begotten." . Husband possessed the power of divorce which was so unlimited and unrestricted that he could divorce his wife whenever he wishes without any lawful ground and could revoked his divorce and divorce again as many times as he favored. He could illogically accuse his wife of falseness, dismiss her and leave her with such infamy as would prevent other suitors; while he himself would go free from any kinds of liability of maintenance or legal punishment. Neither of the wives could get a dower but Islam approves dower as a respect to the wife.. False charges of unchastely were frequently used for depriving the wife from her right of dower. Her protector could deliver her to any person as he wished. But showing respect to women Islam reformed marriage laws in a sweeping and far-reaching way.

Women were considered as material things and where husband were unable to pay his debt during his life time, after his death his creditor would own his wife as reparation . Female child were considered an evil omen and fathers were terrified if the new born baby were female. Fathers not only become unhappy when a female child was born but also felt embarrassed. In pre-Islamic Arabia, there was a ridiculous discrimination against their female children whom they used to bury alive. The Messenger of Allah (peace be upon him) not only protest to this culture but also ordered to stop it. He showing them that supporting their female children would act as a screen for them against the fire of Hell...

Under original Hindu law, women were treated like slave who had no rights of inheritance .If the husband of woman died during her lifetime then she had to burn herself alive when the dead body was cremated. Widow had no right to remarry who had to bear intolerable pain in her daily life. In Chinese culture, there were many atrocious customs had to bear a girl. A male child was treated as an immense gift of God but female was an acceptable degradation. In Greek society, women were treated to be the incarnation of evil and they had no right of inheritance, education, divorce etc.. They were considered as material goods who had no feelings and free will. In ancient Rome, cruelties towards women were unbearable. Women had no rights, dignity or honour and the position of the women was like slave Men had authority to sell her or send her into exile even a husband had power of summarily putting his wife to death for acts like drinking, poisoning and substitution of a spurious child . In Jewish society, women were lived without right, dignity and honour. They had no right of inheritance and were considered as an object owned by the male protector.

Rights, Dignity, Honour and Status of Women in Islam

Islam does not allow the domination of men over women rather it upholds the rights, dignity, honour and status of women by ensuring gender equality and also equality of rights for both male and female in every area of human life. In Islam a woman is completely self-regulating who has legal personality and who is able to enter into contract or can make bequest in her own name. She has right to perform any profession or business and has authority to dispose her property as like as men. She is entitled for inheritance in different capacity like as mother, as wife, as sister and as daughter. She has full freedom to select her husband and also allowed to her dower and maintenance. As the command of Islam to the men is to treat with compassion and full respect to their wives, women are respectable and honourable in Islam. A women as mother has immense respect in Islam than any other person. The holy Quran in many verses commands Muslims to demonstrate respect to their mothers and serve them well even if they left Islam and are still remain as unbelievers. The prophet (peace be upon him) states insistently that the rights of the mother are supreme . In Islam women are most respectable and honorable "if she is a wife, she is life partner, if she is as a mother, the paradise is under the feet of mother, if she is daughter it is blessing of Almighty Allah.

The different types of rights of women ensured in Islam are:

Inheritance

The pre-Islamic customs relating to succession were biased, vindictive, and unreasonable and in most of the cases violated justice . Women were treated as property and they were not entitled to inheritance whether as mother or wife or daughter or sister. There was no specific system for cognates and agnates and always males could get preferences. There were established traditions that the nearest male agnates succeeded to the entire estate of the deceased and females and cognates were excluded. Islam ensured the rights of inheritance of women many centuries ago than western countries , In Islam six classes of persons never deprive from inheritance . Among these six classes of persons, three classes of persons are male (father, husband and son) and rest three are female (mother, wife and daughter). In Islamic law of inheritance, among twelve sharers (called Quranic sharer whose share is define in Quran) numbers of women are eight ("wife, mother, daughter, son's daughter, true grandmother, full sister, consanguine sister and uterine sister") and the numbers of men are four (father, husband, true grandfather and uterine brother) So Islam does not neglect women giving more importance to men.

In case of right of inheritance of a woman as mother three situations may arise. She may be entitle either 1/6 (if the deceased person has a child or son's child how low so ever or two or more brothers or sisters) or 1/3 (if the deceased person do not have any child or son's child or not more than one brother and sister) or 1/3 of residue (if the deceased person have wife or husband and father) (4:11). As wife two situations may arise and she may be entitle either 1/4 (if the deceased person have child or son's child how low so ever) or 1/8 (if the deceased person do not have any child or son's child) of the property of the deceased. (4:12). As daughter, if only one daughter and no son her share is 1/2 and if two or more daughters and no son their share is 2/3 and if there is son daughter will be residue and each daughter will get half of son. (4:11). Besides this, parents could distribute property equally between a son and a daughter. Islam is the only religion that does not deprive women from their right of inheritance rather ensured right of inheritance of women.

Marriage

Allah has created men and women as company for one another and so that they can procreate and live in peace and tranquility according to the commandments of almighty Allah and the directions of His Messenger. Allah says:
"And among His signs is this that He created for you mates from among yourselves, that you may dwell in tranquility with them, and He has put love and mercy between your hearts. Undoubtedly in these are signs for those who reflect.
Marriage is treated as the basis of social life and the beginning of the family life. It is compulsory (Wajib) for a man who has the means to easily pay the dower (Mahr) and to bear the expenses of a wife and children, and also physically fit, and doubts that if does not marry, he may be allured to commit adultery (Zina) and also obligatory for a woman who do not have any other legal way of maintaining herself and who doubts that her sexual urge may move forward her into adultery . It protects society and safe guard human being from foulness and un-chastity . In Islam marriage is an act for the pleasant of Allah because it is according to His orders that husband and wife love each other and help each other to make efforts to continue the human race and rear and foster their children to become true servant of Allah. As it is also the biological instincts

to have sexual intercourse, marriage is not only satisfying sexual lust of men and women but also preserve future generation.

In case of marriage, Islam has given equal importance both bride groom and bride as for being a valid marriage any party may offer to the other party and it must be accepted by the other party. Through valid marriage mutual right of inheritance are established and wife become entitle to her dower and maintenance. But marries does not give power to the husband over the wife's person beyond the limit of law and right upon her goods and property. In marriage in Islam women are at liberty to choose their life partner. Nobody can force her to choose her mate or to marry even one's father, mother, brother, sister or any paternal or maternal guardian. Marriage of major woman previously married without her consent is unanimously void and of a major virgin girl without her consent is unlawful . Islam showed full respect to the women and ensured rights, dignity and honour and equal status of men and women in case of marriage because for being a valid marriage acquiescence of the bride groom as well as bride is mandatory. In this regard no one is superior.

Dower

In pre-Islamic period dower was paid to the wife's father or other guardian, which was used to signify gifts (sadaka) and could therefore be regarded as sell price in present time. Islam approved dower (mahr) to be paid to the wife in case of regular marriage as respect to the wife and not as sell price. Dower may be a sum of money or any other kind of property of which the wife is legally entitled to get from the husband as a token of respect. It cannot be treated as consideration or exchange given to the wife for entering into marriage contract.

Islam has given importance for the payment of dower and also imposed duty on the husband to pay dower to the wife. The holy Quran states, "Give women (wives) their dower with no strings attached. If they themselves (wives) give some of it back to you (waive it), then consume it (dower) with good cheers." (4:4). The Prophet (peace be upon him) said, "Pay dower (mahr) to your wife even it is a ring made of iron" . According to the provision of Islam, husband must have to pay dower to the wife either in cash or any other form and husband has no way to deny his liability except paying dower. It may be prompt or deferred.

It is like a debt or duty for the husband to pay dower and a right of the wife to receive it. In case of dower Islam has showed respect and given full authority to the wife as she can demand her dower at any time without any explanation and can waive full or any part of her dower as she like and no one can interfere in this matter. Islam has given rights to the wife and imposed duty on the husband if the amount of dower was not settled during the time of marriage or later on, the wife is entitled to proper dower, though the marriage was completed on the stipulation that the wife cannot demand any dower. In determine the amount of proper dower, the social position of the wife's family, financial condition of the husband, personal qualifications of the bride and dower settled upon the female members of the family of the bride's father will be consider. Under Islamic law, where there is a marriage there is a dower whatever may be the amount and it is bridal gift . According to the direction of the Prophet (peace be upon him) if anybody do not pay the dower in the Day of Judgment he will be treated as adulterate. Islam has ensured the right of dower of a woman and given her unlimited and unrestricted power to dispose her dower in any lawful way as she like.

Maintenance

Maintenance (nafaqa) is very significant issue in Muslim personal law. To afford maintenance is not only legally approved but also it is an act of devotion (ibadat). Under Muslim law, maintenance is due to the wife from the husband as a recompense for the matrimonial restraint and is one of the necessary and inherent conditions of the marriage contract. Husband responsibility is to provide proper maintenance and it is such a duty that must be discharged cheerfully without any censure, hurt or patronization . The holy command "Let him provide her (wife) maintenance according to his ability". (65:7). It is duty upon the husband to provide proper food, cloth and accommodation if she surrenders herself to him although she is Muslim or infidel or poor or rich, grown-up or young .

Muslim husband is legally bound to provide maintenance to his wife so long as she is truthful to him and observe his lawful orders whether she is poor or rich will not be considered. Maintenance is one of important legal rights of the wife and a legal duty of the husband who will not be exempted from this liability whatever may be his financial condition. A wife can demand maintenance during her sickness in her husband's house and even if a man divorces his wife her bread and accommodation are attributed upon him during the period of iddat (remaining unmarried for a period of three months after dissolution of marriage) whether the divorce is of reversible or irreversible kind. The wife becomes entitle for maintenance immediately after valid marriage and husband cannot deny his liability of providing maintenance. When there subsists a valid marriage there must have a right of maintenance by the wife. Islam does not impose liability upon the wife to bear expenses of the family or to bear expenses of her husband on any condition rather ensured her right to get maintenance from her husband.

In Bangladesh currently there are two statutes containing provisions regarding the maintenance of wife. Section 5 of the Family Courts Ordinance, 1985 (Ordinance No- XVIII of 1985) states that every family court is competent to entertain, try and dispose of any suit relating to the dower and maintenance of a woman. Section 9 of the Muslim Family Laws Ordinance, 1961 (Ordinance No- VIII of 1961) runs: “If any husband fails to maintain his wife adequately or where there are more wives than one, fails to maintain them equitably, the wife or all or any of the wives may, in addition to seeking any other legal remedy available, apply to the chairman who shall constitute an arbitration council to determine the matter, and the arbitration council may issue a certificate specifying the amount which shall be paid as maintenance by the husband and the amount fixed by the council is recoverable as arrears of land revenue. Of course, an aggrieved party may prefer an appeal to the court of assistant judge whose decision is final and no appeal shall lie in any court of law.”

Divorce

In the Dark Age, when Islam does not emerge in Arabs, only the husband had power of divorce and which was so unrestricted and unlimited that he practiced in the most inhuman ways. Husband could divorce his wife whenever he like without any legal or reasonable cause. He had also the power to revoke his divorce and divorce again as many times as he favored. He could, moreover, if he so desired, swear that he had made no sexual relation with his wife, though still living with her. The husband exercised limitless rights over the wife. If a man became angry with his wife, whether for any reasonable cause or just to satisfy his caprice, he could divorce her at once, but the unfortunate wife could neither have recourse to any legal procedure nor get any maintenance from him nor claim any other kind of right from him. Regarding right of divorce men enjoyed vast powers who could easily get rid of his wife by leveling a flimsy charge against him.

The Prophet (peace be upon him) looked upon these evil customs of divorce with tremendous dissatisfaction and regarded their practice as considered to damage the foundation of society. It was quite impossible to abolish this evil custom completely. The Prophet (peace be upon him) had to mould the mind of an uncultured and semi-barbarous community to a higher development. In case of extreme emergency, Islam permitted divorce if all efforts of bringing together have unsuccessful. Islam recognized that when it has become impossible to continue conjugal life it is better for both husband and wife to separate harmoniously rather than miserably bound together which turns the home into a hell.

The rectification of Prophet Mohammad marked a new departure in the history of Eastern legislation. He reserved unrestricted power of divorce by the husband but also given to the wife the right of obtaining the partition on rational grounds. Though divorce is allowed in Islam with some conditions it discourages dissolution of a marriage-tie as Prophet (peace be upon him) says: "Of all things that Islam has permitted, divorce is the most hated by Allah..

Islam has given to the women right regarding dissolution of marriage by:

1) Delegated divorce (Talaque-e-tafweez):

Though the husband possesses primarily the power of divorce wife also may exercise this right to dissolve her marriage if the husband delegates the power of dissolution of marriage to the wife . This delegation of power can be during the marriage or at any time after marriage. The power so delegated to the wife is irrevocable and it can be exercised even after the institution of a suit by the husband against her for restitution of conjugal rights.

2) Redemption (Khul'a):

It means a mutual agreement between husband and wife where both of them agree to break off their marriage in lieu of a recompense paid by the wife to her husband out of her property . If the relationship of a husband and a wife is not fine, the wife has a right to seek divorce (khul'a) by renouncing her claim to the dower. According to the Prophet (Saw) of Islam, "If a woman be prejudiced by a marriage, let it be broken.

3) Mutual release (Mubar'at): When both the parties of a marriage feel aversion, they have liberty to release each other without any claim upon the other. In this form of divorce both of the parties to the marriage has right to offer and the other party has right to accept and when it is accepted marriage will be dissolved and it is an irrevocable divorce.

Right to Choose Profession

In Islam like men women have various responsibilities towards the family and society as she is considered one of the two important pillars of the society. Islam does not like laziness, vanity and workless people. In Islam there is no difference between men and women in regard to work and working is a duty for both. In Islam women have freedom to choose their occupation but in choosing their profession they must keep in mind that they have some limitations due to their physical structure. As they are exquisite, sensitive beautiful beings they have to be more conscious before involving any profession. Though in Islam women have liberty to select their profession but it impose some restrictions at the same time because a married woman cannot choose any profession by which her husband will be deprived to enjoy his conjugal rights or children will be deprived from maternal love, care and affection and proper education and training.

Right to Proprietorship
In regard to ownership of property

Islam has given equal respect to the women like men. She may gain property through lawful means and become owner and she has also right to dispose of that property in any legal way as she wishes. Nobody whether father or husband or mother or even her children have no right to interfere her regarding her property. It is not her responsibility to bear expense of the family even her maintenance or maintenance of the children. Husband has no right in her personal property. She is not liable to pay the debt of her husband. But in case of necessity he may take loan from her and in that case she will have all rights of a creditor.

Right to Seek Knowledge

In Islam acquiring knowledge is obligatory for both men and women. In this regard an unmarried woman has full freedom to acquire knowledge and nobody can obstruct her from acquiring knowledge. A married woman also has right of acquiring knowledge but she must observe the right of her husband and children.

Right to Involve in Politics

Islam ensured political independence of men and women. There is opportunity for a woman to involve in politics . She can participate in political convention, street demonstrations, congregations and Friday prayers. She has right to self defense and defends her property and even she can participate in war to defend the sovereignty of her own country. But for all these she has to follow the directions of Islam.

Right to Choose Residence

A woman has freedom to choose residence for herself. In Islam, as it is the liability of husband to provide proper maintenance to his wife, a married woman must stay to her husband's place of residence. Considering the ability and benefit of her husband a married woman can select her residence in such place as dignity of the family is properly maintained. According to the direction of Islam she cannot claim her residence in such place which will be some hardship for her husband.

Economic Rights of Women

A Muslim woman is allowed to involve herself in economic activities following some rules. The women who are highly talented and have the opportunity to acquire higher degree can render services for the betterment of the society, particularly in the teaching profession. But here too, a strict Islamic code of conduct has to be observed in the classroom. As for medical profession, women doctors are badly needed in the field of gynecology and obstetrics. Usually women feel shy and even forbidden by Islam from consulting male doctor as per as possible in their ante-natal and post-natal treatment but if it is a question of life and death then in special circumstances it is permitted. In Islam women are encourages in medical profession. Women can involve in welfare institutions of the society. With her Allah-given touch of loving and affection she can handle juvenile delinquents, drop-outs from schools frustrated youths. Even she has right to work in a factory if it is run by women.

Woman is not forbidden to go out of her home for necessity. In the time of the Prophet (peace be upon him), women went out to the market or their farms. The prophet (peace be upon him) did not stop a woman in her iddat from going out of her house in case of necessity. Jabir ibn Abdullah says husband of my aunt divorced her and when she was spending her iddat in the house she wanted to go outside of the house to get some of her date palms harvested and sold. Someone halted her, saying that you are not allowed to go out of the house during iddat. She went to the Prophet (peace be upon him) to whether she could go outside of the house or not and the Prophet (peace be upon him) said, "You go out and get the date trees harvested (and sold) so that you may be able to do some other good work...

Prevailing Misconceptions in Bangladesh Regarding Women Rights in Islam

Some misconceptions regarding women's rights in Islam are prevailing in Bangladesh for long time. These misconceptions directly neglect the women, dishonored them and discriminate them. Some people without proper religious knowledge, to dominate the women, to deprive women from their rights as given in Islam and to establish superiority of men over women practice these misconceptions as rule of Islam. But Islam does not support these misconceptions these are direct contradiction of Islamic rules and principles. Some misconceptions regarding women rights prevailing in Bangladesh are:

1) "Islam deprived women as in inheritance they are getting half share as compared to men". There is a misconception in Bangladesh that Islam deprived women in case of right of inheritance. But most of the people do not realize what the place of women in Islam is. In Islam, from the property of her parents a woman is entitled to get 1/2 of the share as compared to her brother but she has no financial liability towards the family. She is entitled to her dower, to get gifts during her marriage and she is not required to spend her income to bear the expenses of the family. Her all expenses are bear by father before marriage and by the husband after marriage Besides these, she has right of inheritance in the property of her husband and also in the property of the children.

2) "Unconditionally a man can take four wives at a time".

Another misconception prevailing in Bangladesh regarding polygamy. According to the rules of Islam, maximum four wives might be taken by a man at one time only when he possessed the strength of character to deal justly with them. The holy Quran says:
"If you fear that you will not able to deal justly with the orphans, marry women of your choice, two or three or four; but if you fear that you will not be able to deal justly with them, then only one.
The above rule on polygamy is conditional. The verse specially refers to the justice to be done to orphans. It was revealed immediately after the Battle Uhud when the Muslim community was left with many orphans and widows and some captives-of-war. The treatment was to be governed by principles of greatest humanity and equality. If a man wants to take more than one wife he should have sufficient financial resources to look after the needs of the additional wives that he has taken and he must do equal justice with them in regard to the fulfillment of their conjugal and other rights . The logic to justify polygamy is that it prevents divorce of the sick, older and barren wife and to refrains men from extra-marital relationship and also remove social hypocrisy

3) "Consent of bride is not so important for marriage". Male dominated societies of Bangladesh do not want to give equal importance of the consent of bride like bride groom in case of marriage. They think that consent of the father or guardian is final for the marriage of a girl but Islam does not support it. According to Islam, for a valid marriage free consent of the bride and bride groom is required. Islam has given right of a woman to choose her life partner.

4) "No marriage without dowry". The most heinous

practice in Bangladesh which Islam never supports is dowry system. It has become such social practice in Bangladesh that sometimes marriage cannot imagine without dowry. Some greedy people established system in the society that wife have to bring wealth from her parents and sometimes they torture physically or mentally and even sometimes causes death of the wife by torture for dowry.

5) “Women have no right of divorce in Islam”. Though in Islam husband has absolute power to divorce but he may delegates this power to the wife. According to Islam both husband and wife can separate by mutual understanding. Besides these, she may demand separation by relinquishing all claims to the husband.

The main reasons of prevailing misconceptions in Bangladesh regarding women rights in is Islam are firstly not having proper knowledge regarding rules and regulations of Islam; secondly to dominate the women and to establish superiority of men over women; thirdly to deprive the women from their legal rights as given them by Islam; fourthly illiteracy of women and lack of awareness among women are one of the main reasons of misconceptions regarding women rights in Islam; fifthly to neglect the women and to dishonor them and to discriminate them; as most of the religious interpreters are male.

Conclusion

Islam is the complete and comprehensive code of life which covers all aspects of human life from cradle to grave. Allah has created both male and female for worship and thralldom and to play distinct roles in the society but there is no superiority between them except on the ground of morality. Islam has guaranteed the rights of women in every sphere of life like men. It is only the religious which does not discriminate between men and women. It also does not allow the domination of men over women. In the Dark Age, when women were treated as material things and who had no rights and if the husband of a woman died during her lifetime, then she had to burn herself alive when the dead body was cremated and then Islam not only protected the women but also gave them right, dignity and honour. Islam does not impose any financial liability on the women rather ensuring her right of dower, maintenance and inheritance. Islam does not treat women "an instrument of the Devil". In Islam, she has freedom to involve herself in any social and economic activities and even in politics. But in male dominated society of Bangladesh, some misconceptions are prevailing regarding women rights in Islam due to lack of proper religious knowledge, lack of awareness of women regarding their rights as given in Islam, the prevailing customs and also for dominating mentality of men. Sometimes to deprive the women or to dishonor the women or to blaspheme the women or for financial interest or for political interest, men practice some bad customs and claim these are the rules of Islam but Islam never supports these bad practices. Due to the lack of proper Islamic knowledge, sometimes women also blamed the Islam injustice to them or dishonored them or deprived them. To know the rights of women in Islam and to understand the actual position of women in Islam and to eliminate the prevailing misconceptions regarding women's rights in Islam, proper Islamic knowledge and awareness of women is essential and also necessary to change the dominating mentality of the men.

CHAPTER FOUR

Myths and Realities about Women

While negative stereotypes of Muslims in the media are perpetuated, they ultimately contribute to skewed perceptions about Islam, and more specifically, Muslim women. The effects of Islamophobia are also being seen in Europe, as many nations are acting on their misdirected understanding of Islam by moving to ban burqa and niqab in the hopes of liberating Muslim women from the "oppression of Islam". But what negative media portrayals of Islam have also contributed to are myths that hold no factual basis. For example, the idea that Muslim women are unequal to men, is untrue. On the contrary, Islam extends similar rights to women that are equal to those of men. The general idea that Muslim women have no right to lead and direct their own lives is completely false. In actuality, Muslim women have the right to possess property, gain education, seek employment and participate in both political and social life. They can also keep their maiden names after marriage. It's also important to consider the fact that while when Western women had to earn equality after suffrage, Muslim women were given these rights from the beginning without any struggle.

The aim of this topic are to challenge and point out the inaccuracy in the deeply held beliefs about Muslims, and Muslim women in particular, and to provide facts based on quotes from the Qur'an itself.

1. Myth: Hijab is a form of women's subjugation

To dress appropriately and cover one's body is obligated for women, so that they will not be sexually objectified and looked down upon. They should be respected for their intelligence, etiquettes and other aspects of their personalities. Hijab also encompasses modesty and chastity:

"O Prophet! Tell your wives and your daughters and the women of the believers to draw their cloaks (veils) all over their bodies (i.e. screen themselves completely except the eyes or one eye to see the way). That will be better, that they should be known (as free respectable women) so as not to be molested. And Allah is Ever Oft Forgiving, Most Merciful." [Qur'an 33:59]

This type of modest dress has been worn by righteous non-Muslim women throughout history. Prominent examples are traditional Catholic Nuns, Mother Teresa and the Virgin Mary, mother of Jesus. Hijab is also mandatory for men, so that they can preserve their chastity. Men are also obliged to dress modestly. Another form of hijab for them is to lower their gazes and avoid looking at women lustily.

"Say to the believing men that they should lower their sight and guard their private parts; that will make for greater purity for them. Indeed Allâh is well acquainted with all that they do." [Qur'an 24:30]

2. Myth: Women hold a lower status in Islam

Islam holds women in highest regard in every phase of her life: "when she is a daughter, she opens a door of Jannah (Heaven) for her father. When she is a wife, she completes half of the Deen (Religion) of her husband. When she is a mother, Jannah (Heaven) lies under her feet."

The men are required to treat women with honor and respect in all circumstances.

The Prophet (P.B.U.H.) said, "None but a noble man treats women in an honorable manner, and none but an ignorant man treats women disgracefully."

The status of the mother is three times higher than of the father:

A man came to the Messenger (P.B.U.H.) and asked, "O Messenger of God! Who among the people is the most worthy of my good companionship? The Prophet (P.B.U.H.) said: 'Your mother.' The man said: 'Then who?' The Prophet (P.B.U.H.) said: 'Then your mother.' The man further asked: 'Then who?' The Prophet (P.B.U.H.) said: "Then your mother.' The man asked again: 'Then who?' The Prophet (P.B.U.H.) said: 'Then your father.'"

Allah has honored women greatly. He has honored them as daughters, mothers and wives and given them rights and virtues and has enjoined good treatment in ways that are not shared by men in many cases.

A Muslim woman also has the authority to voice her opinions. The Prophet's wives would debate with him, and this set an example for the wives in all generations.

It is narrated that the women of the Sahaabah used to argue and debate with them, and indeed this is the way in which the Mothers of the Believers [i.e., the Prophet's wives] used to act with our Prophet (P.B.U.H.). As 'Umar ibn al-Khattaab said to the Prophet (P.B.U.H.):

"We Quraysh used to control our women, but when we came to the Ansaar we found that they were a people who were controlled by their women. So our women started to adopt the ways of the Ansaari women. I got angry with my wife and she argued with me and I did not like her arguing with me. She said, 'Why do you object to me arguing with you? By Allah, the wives of the Prophet (P.B.U.H.) argue with him...'" [Narrated by al-Bukhaari, 4895; Muslim, 1479]

3. Myth: Education is forbidden for women

To gain knowledge is an obligation for every Muslim man and woman, so that they can fulfill their religious and social responsibilities. Plus, it is the husband's responsibility to have his wife educated if this was neglected at her parents' home.

"Seeking knowledge is compulsory for each and every Muslim (i.e. both male and female)."

Islamic scholars have agreed that when the word, "Muslim" is mentioned in the Qur'an, it is in reference to both the genders. Seeking knowledge is not limited only on religious studies but it is encouraged for both men and women to learn worldly science as well.

In Islam, both men and women are equally encouraged and rewarded to educate themselves and learn what suit their needs and nature. The Prophet (P.B.U.H) used to fix a special day to teach women their religious matters apart from men.

The Messenger of Allah said: "...Whoever follows a path in pursuit of knowledge, Allah will make easy for him a path

to Paradise."
In fact, Islam gives knowledgeable people higher ranks and recognition than others who are not.
"Allah will exalt those of you who believe, and those who are given knowledge, in high degrees; and Allah is Aware of what you do." [Quran 58:11]

4. Myth: A Muslim woman has no share in Inheritance.

One of the misconceptions about Islam is that it is unjust because it gives men double the share of inheritance. Actually, this is due to the fact that men are responsible for taking care of his wife, children, parents and other relatives. Therefore, it is sometimes necessary that men are given higher preference.
"For men is a share of what the parents and close relatives leave, and for women is a share of what the parents and close relatives leave, be it little or much, an obligatory share." [Qur'an 4:7]

There are three types of shares for a woman's inheritance:
1. A woman will have an equal share as that of the man. 2. A woman will have an equal share as that of the man, or a little less. 3. A woman's share will be half of the man.

It is understood that the minimum inheritance willed to the woman should be half, and the bequest is hers alone and the husband has no say in it:

"O You who believe! You are forbidden to inherit women against their will, and you should not treat them with harshness, that you may take away part of the Mahr (bridal-money given by the husband to his wife at time of marriage) you have given them, unless they commit open illegal sexual intercourse. And live with them honorably. If you dislike them, it may be that you dislike a thing and Allah brings through it a great deal of good." [Qur'an 4:19]

It is clear from the aforementioned quote from the the Qur'an that women are to be given their rights to inheritance.

In this passage men are forbidden to take their partner's assests at all unless a crime (adultery) is committed, and even then the portion to be taken is small in comparison. Further, men must act honorably and justly with their spouses, as their relationship is from Allah and is inherently good.

5. Myth: Honor Killing is justified

The Qur'an does not talk about "honor killing". In fact, there is no Islamic evidence that would justify it. What has been termed as "honor killing" describes incidents that are inflicted on both men and women. Murders of innocents and civilians occur throughout every part of the world, however, the myth that is perpetuated is that murder is not only condoned in Islam, but that it is common practice. In actuality, there are Fatwas and political campaigns against murder of innocents across the Muslim world.

The Qur'an upholds the right and sanctity of life as the most basic form of human rights, and it condemns the killings of innocents:

"That if anyone slays a human being – unless it be [in punishment] for murder or for spreading corruption on earth – it shall be as though he had slain all mankind; whereas, if anyone saves a life, it shall be as though he had saved the lives of all mankind." [Qur'an 5:32]

Killing a Muslim unlawfully is a serious matter and a grave crime. Allah says that a person who commits cold blooded murder shall not be pardoned and will enter Hell:

"And whoever kills a believer intentionally, his recompense is Hell to abide therein; and the Wrath and the Curse of Allah are upon him, and a great punishment is prepared for him." [Qur'an 4:93]

The Messenger of Allah (P.B.U.H.) said: "The believer will continue to be encompassed by the mercy of Allah so long as he does not shed blood that it is forbidden to shed."

To sum up, Islam has given tremendous rights and protection to women, so they will not be ill-treated in the hands of men and/or society at large. The Prophet (P.B.U.H.) highly respected women and advised men to treat women kindly and generously. Men and women both are viewed equally in the eyes of Allah, but because they are two different beings, they are given separate responsibilities. Based on these principles, the man is not better than the woman or vice-versa in the Islamic way of life.......

CHAPTER FIVE

True importance and Education of women

The first person to embrace Islam was a woman; Khadija (ra).
The greatest scholar of Islam was a woman; Aisha (ra).
The person who loved the Prophet (saw) the most was a woman; Fatima (ra).

Despite misconceptions, the status of women in Islam is that of a beloved equal. In the midst of a deeply sexist historical context, the Prophet (saw) preached boldly on the importance of women; celebrating their unique contributions to family and society, condemning the ill-treatment of women and campaigning for their rights.

Many of the negative stereotypes around women in Islam arise not from Islamic guidance but from cultural practices, which not only denigrate the rights and experiences of women, but also stand in direct opposition to the teachings of Allah (swt) and His Prophet (saw).

Far from the stereotype of the voiceless and veiled Muslim woman, Shaykh Ibn Baaz argues, "There is no doubt that Islam came to honour to the woman, guard her, protect her from the wolves of mankind, secure her rights and raise her status."

With all the confusion between history, culture and religion, it's important to ask ourselves the question; what do the Qur'an and the Ahadith actually teach us about the status of women in Islam?

What Islam teaches us about gender equality

The Qur'an teaches us that Adam and Eve were created from the same soul; both equally guilty, equally responsible and equally valued. As Muslims, we believe that all human beings are born in a pure state – men and women – and that we must strive to preserve this purity through faith, as well as good intentions and deeds.

The theme of equality runs through other Islamic teachings, too. An important verse in the Qur'an reads, "The men believers and the women believers are responsible for each other. They enjoin the good and forbid the evil, they observe prayers and give charitable alms and obey God and his Prophet." (Qur'an, 9:71).

This verse shows us that men and women have equal responsibilities for observing Islamic teachings; another Quranic verse lays out the status of women and men as equals, stating, "To whoever, male or female, does good deeds and has faith, we shall give a good life and reward them according to the best of their actions." (16:97)

Protecting women's rights

In 610 CE, the Prophet Muhammad (saw) was living in historical context rooted in sexism. From Europe to the Arabic world, women were not treated as equal to men.

Islam itself was born in the Arabian Peninsula, now Saudi Arabia, where women did not have businesses, own property or inherit money. What's more, forced marriage was common, education for girls was rare, and female babies were often abandoned or buried alive.

The Prophet (saw), and his businesswoman wife, Khadija (ra), stood against many of these unjust practices, advocating for men to treat women and girls with the utmost respect. According to the laws of Islam, all life is considered sacred, and men and women have the right to choose whom to marry and should never be forced.

Under Islamic laws, women also have the right to sell and buy properties, run businesses, demand her dowry at any point during her marriage, vote and take an active part in all aspects of politics and society. It is notable that many Islamic countries, such as Turkey and Pakistan, have had female Presidents.

The Prophet (saw) also promoted equal access to education, teaching us that, "The pursuit of knowledge is a duty of every Muslim, man and woman." [Ibn Maja] The Beloved's (saw) own daughter, Fatima (ra), was highly educated and respected. It is documented that whenever Fatima (ra) entered a room, the Prophet (saw) would stand up, and give his seat to her.

A legacy of female empowerment

As Muslims, we strive to follow the Sunnah and continue the great works of the Prophet (saw). That includes advocating and working for the millions of women around the world who are still victims of systematic oppression and violence.

Our Women's Welfare appeal is a charity that supports

women, through a variety of tailored projects. We empower women and girls around the world through education, domestic abuse support services, dignity kits, safe spaces for refugee women and sustainable vocational training, such as training in sewing and setting up textiles businesses, and climate-resistant farming.

> "
>
> *Give to charity for women in need, and you will be building upon the legacy of the Prophet (saw) and the many incredible Muslim women who have fought for the rights of women and girls, for generations.*
>
> *Champion women and girls by donating to charity for women in need, and help even more women to thrive and follow in the footsteps of Khadija (ra), Aisha (ra) and Fatima (ra)!*"

Women and Education in IsLam

Gender inequality is a common accusation made against Islam and a disparity in educational opportunities between men and women in many Muslim countries is often cited as a primary example of this. Education is seen as one of the pivotal factors in determining the economic, social and political advancement of a society and if, those making up over fifty percent of that society, are denied such a basic fundamental right then needless to say human rights activists will seek to find reasons for this disparity. Religion, particularly Islam is cited as a major stumbling block for women's advancement. Studies have shown that in many parts of Africa and South East Asia women's acquisition of knowledge is either fervently opposed; regulated to secondary importance as compared to men or encumbered with so many restrictions as to make it almost impossible for female students to acquire a decent standard of education.

This is a sad reflection upon Muslims and the societies that we have built since knowledge is one of the important pillars upon which the edifice of Islam has been raised. The very fact that the first revelation upon the Holy Prophet (blessings and peace be upon him) contained the commandment to 'read' speaks volumes of the emphasis Islam lays on education. Within Islam there is no disagreement found on acquisition of knowledge being binding and obligatory. The importance and excellence of knowledge has been highlighted both directly and indirectly in over five hundred places in the Holy Qur'an. Indeed one of the essential duties and responsibilities of Prophethood was the dissemination of knowledge and wisdom to all. Allah Almighty says:

كَمَآ أَرْسَلْنَا فِيكُمْ رَسُولاً مِّنكُمْ يَتْلُوا۟ عَلَيْكُمْ ءَايَـٰتِنَا وَيُزَكِّيكُمْ وَيُعَلِّمُكُمُ □لْكِتَـٰبَ(
وَ□لْحِكْمَةَ وَيُعَلِّمُكُم مَّا لَمْ تَكُونُوا۟ تَعْلَمُونَ)

Likewise, We have sent you (Our) Messenger (blessings and peace be upon him) from amongst yourselves who recites to you Our Revelations and purifies and sanctifies (your hearts and ill-commanding selves) and teaches you the Book and inculcates in you logic and wisdom and enlightens you (on the mysteries of spiritual gnosis and divine truth) which you did not know. [al-Baqara, 2:151.]

هُوَ □لَّذِى بَعَثَ فِى □لْأُمِّيِّـۧنَ رَسُولاً مِّنْهُمْ يَتْلُوا۟ عَلَيْهِمْ ءَايَـٰتِهِۦ وَيُزَكِّيهِمْ وَيُعَلِّمُهُمُ(
□لْكِتَـٰبَ وَ□لْحِكْمَةَ وَإِن كَانُوا۟ مِن قَبْلُ لَفِى ضَلَـٰلٍ مُّبِينٍ)

He is the One Who sent a (Glorious) Messenger (blessings and peace be upon him) amongst the illiterate people from amongst themselves who recites to them His Revelations and cleanses and purifies them (outwardly and inwardly) and teaches them the Book and wisdom. Indeed, they were in open error before (his most welcome arrival). [al-Jumu'a, 62:2.]

A basic principle of Islamic Shariah states that when a commandment is revealed, even if the masculine form of word is used the female gender is also included in this commandment. If this principle is rejected then the basic pillars of Islam such as prayer, fasting, pilgrimage and alms-due will become null and void for women. So though God Almighty and the Holy Prophet (blessings and peace be upon him) use the masculine form of sentence to describe most of the commandments, women are also bound to act and follow those rules and regulations.

The study of these verses clearly shows that the prophetic responsibilities of Prophet Muhammad (blessings and peace be upon him) through his Prophethood included recital of the verses, purgation of the self, education of the Book and wisdom and communication of knowledge. Four duties out of five directly talk of knowledge whereas the second and fifth in the sequence refers to a particular kind of knowledge, which is technically defined as mysticism or sufism. However if the doors of acquiring knowledge are closed for women or unjustified restrictions are imposed upon this acquisition, which religion will they act upon? How can they come to know the nature of the verses that have been revealed to them? How will they attain the wisdom and hikma that Allah Almighty wished them to know through the Holy Prophet (blessings and peace be upon him)? How are they to teach the fundamentals of the faith to their children if they have no knowledge of it themselves?

The Holy Qur'an also states:

)قُلْ هَلْ يَسْتَوِى الَّذِينَ يَعْلَمُونَ وَالَّذِينَ لاَ يَعْلَمُونَ إِنَّمَا يَتَذَكَّرُ أُوْلُواْ الأَلْبَـــٰـبِ(

Say: 'Can those who have knowledge and those who do not be alike?' So only the wise do receive the admonition. [al-Zumar, 39:9.]

)إِنَّمَا يَخْشَى اللَّهَ مِنْ عِبَادِهِ الْعُلَمَـــٰـؤُاْ إِنَّ اللَّهَ عَزِيزٌ غَفُورٌ(

So only those of His servants who have knowledge (of these realities with a vision and outlook) fear Him. Surely, Allah is Almighty, Most Forgiving. [Fatir, 35:28.]

None of these verses specify that only 'wise men' receive admonition or that only 'male servants' who have knowledge fear Him. If reference to the importance of knowledge has not been restricted within the purview of men by Almighty God, why do we persevere in creating them ourselves? A number of Prophetic traditions also talk directly about knowledge being obligatory and binding in character.

The Holy Prophet (blessings and peace be upon him) said:

«طَلَبُ الْعِلْمِ فَرِيضَةٌ عَلَى كُلِّ مُسْلِمٍ».

Acquisition of knowledge is binding on all Muslims (both men and women without any discrimination). [Narrated by Ibn Maja in al-Sunan, 1:81 §224.]

The Holy Prophet (blessings and peace be upon him) also said at another place:

«أُطْلُبُوا الْعِلْمَ وَلَوْ بِالصِّينِ».

Acquire knowledge even if you may have to go to China for it. [Narrated by al-Bazzar in al-Musnad, 1:175 §95.]

He (blessings and peace be upon him) said at another place:

«مَنْ سَلَكَ طَرِيقًا يَلْتَمِسُ فِيهِ عِلْمًا سَهَّلَ اللهُ لَهُ بِهِ طَرِيقًا إِلَى الْجَنَّةِ».

Allah Almighty makes the path to paradise easier for him

who walks on it for getting knowledge. [Narrated by Muslim in al-Sahih, 4:2074 &2699.]

It is apparent from the Holy Qur'an and hadiths that the acquisition of knowledge is obligatory for women in the same way as in the case of men. The study of the life of the Holy Prophet (blessings and peace be upon him) also shows that he himself made special arrangements for the education and training of women.

Abu Sa'id al-Khudri reports that some women said to the Holy Prophet (blessings and peace be upon him): 'men have gone ahead of us (in terms of acquisition of knowledge). Therefore, appoint a special day for our benefit as well.' The Holy Prophet (blessings and peace be upon him) fixed one day for them. He (blessings and peace be upon him) would meet them on that day, advise them and educate them about commandments of Allah Almighty. [Narrated by al-Bukhari in al-Sahih, 1:50.]

'A'isha al-Siddiqa, mother of the faithful, was a hadith-narrator, scholar, intellectual and jurist of great standing. She is believed to have reported 2,210 traditions. Abu Hurayra, 'Abd Allah b. 'Amr and Anas b. Malik (may Allah be well pleased with them) were the only ones from amongst male hadith-narrators who had narrated more traditions than she did. This itself illustrates that women could not only teach women but also men after fulfilling certain preconditions.

'A'isha bint Talha (may Allah be well pleased with her) reports:

I stayed with 'A'isha. People from every city would come to me including the old ones (who would put forward questions) because they knew that I am her servant. And the students who were young would treat me like their sister and would present gifts (to 'A'isha through me). Many would also write me letters (so that I could reply them back after soliciting answers from 'A'isha. I would submit: O aunt! Mr so and so has written a letter and there is his present as well. 'A'isha would say in reply to this: O daughter! Answer his query and give him present in exchange as well. If you have nothing to give, let me know, I will give. So she would return (the present in exchange and I would send it back along with the letter). [Narrated by al-Bukhari in al-Adab al-Mufrad.

It is important to note here that the concept of knowledge in Islam covers a broad spectrum of subjects. All interpreters of the Holy Qur'an are in agreement that the first five verses of chapter al-'Alaq form the beginning of the sending of revelation:

□قرَأ بِ□سْمِ رَبِّكَ □لذِى خلَقَ. خلَقَ □لإِنسَـٰـنَ مِنْ علَقٍ. □قرَأ ورَبُّكَ □لأكرَمُ.(
(□لذِى علَّمَ بِ□لقلَمِ. علَّمَ □لإِنسَـٰـنَ مَا لَمْ يَعْلَمْ

(O Beloved!) Read (commencing) with the Name of Allah, Who has created (everything). He created man from a hanging mass (clinging) like a leech (to the mother's womb). Read, and your Lord is Most Generous, Who taught man (reading and writing) by the pen, Who (besides that) taught man (all that) which he did not know. [al-'Alaq, 96:1–5.]

The first commandment contained in these verses relates to 'reading' as a part of a process of acquisition of knowledge. In addition to the description of Allah Almighty being the Creator and Sustainer, two branches of knowledge are mentioned, embryology and sociology.

Whilst indicating knowledge of biology and morality in these verses, the Qur'an explains the Islamic concept of knowledge as being very vast.

Acquisition of knowledge embraces within in its fold all of its branches, both religious and secular, which are productive for mankind. It is important to note that this is not restricted to the purview of the traditional religious sciences. Instead many verses of the Holy Qur'an invite man to ponder and meditate over the creation of the universe. Thus it would be wrong to allow women to just partake in learning of the religious sciences and prohibit her from gaining a wider scope in her learning.

Another misnomer is the view that suggests women are only allowed to gain knowledge from female teachers and that instruction from men is prohibited due to the demands of purdah. Although an ideal environment would dictate women teaching women, we do not live in an ideal world where this is always possible. Since Islam is a religion for all nations and all times, it is based on practical reality. There is no stipulation that only women can teach other women or a bar regarding male teachers for women. If the rules of attire and dress are properly observed then men can teach female students under Sharia. This is also apparent from the above mentioned hadith where the Holy Prophet (blessings and peace be upon him) himself made arrangements for the education and training of women where one day was particularly specified for women in the Prophet's Mosque.

Indeed those who quote the verses of the Holy Qur'an regarding the veil as an argument against women leaving the home in pursuit of knowledge are also severely misguided. If attending a school or college in the pursuit of knowledge constitutes breaking the laws of purdah then anytime a women steps out of her home would entail the same breakage of laws. This would of course create a ludicrous situation where a woman could never leave her home for any reason. If one looks at the verses regarding the veil Allah Almighty states:

وَقُل لِّلْمُؤْمِنَـٰتِ يَغْضُضْنَ مِنْ أَبْصَـٰرِهِنَّ وَيَحْفَظْنَ فُرُوجَهُنَّ وَلَا يُبْدِينَ زِينَتَهُنَّ(
)إِلَّا مَا ظَهَرَ مِنْهَا

And direct the believing women that they (too) must keep their eyes lowered and guard their chastity, and must not show off their adornments and beautification except that (part of it) which becomes visible itself. [al-Nur, 24:31.]

يَـٰٓأَيُّهَا □لنَّبِىُّ قُل لِّأَزْوَاجِكَ وَبَنَاتِكَ وَنِسَآءِ □لْمُؤْمِنِينَ يُدْنِينَ عَلَيْهِنَّ مِن(
)جَلَـٰبِيبِهِنَّ ذَالِكَ أَدْنَىٰٓ أَن يُعْرَفْنَ فَلَا يُؤْذَيْنَ وَكَانَ □للَّهُ غَفُورًا رَّحِيمًا

O Prophet! Say to your wives, your daughters and the women of believers that, (whilst going out,) they should draw their veils as coverings over them. It is more likely that this way they may be recognized (as pious, free women), and may not be hurt (considered by mistake as roving slave girls). And Allah is Most Forgiving, Ever-Merciful. [12 al-Ahzab, 33:59.]

Neither of these verses prohibits a woman leaving her house. In fact they merely stipulate that when she leaves the house she should observe the veil whilst outside. Indeed these commandments are themselves a great justification for women stepping out of their homes and becoming active members within society. Moreover if the act of a woman stepping out of her home was prohibited, why did the revered wives of the Holy Prophet (blessings and peace be upon him) participate in battles? If we study the following traditions we come to know the range of functions women performed during the period of Prophethood.

Anas b. Malik (may Allah be well pleased with him) narrates: when people became separated from the Holy Prophet (blessings and peace be upon him), I saw 'A'isha bint Abi Bakr and Umm Sulaym (may Allah be well pleased with them) were completely covered in attire. They would bring water-bags upon their back, offer it to the thirsty Muslims and then return. They would bring water-bags again and made the thirsty Muslims drink it. [Narrated by al-Bukhari in al-Sahih, 3:1055 §2724.]

Umm 'Atiya (may Allah be well pleased with her) says: I participated in six battles with the Holy Prophet (blessings and peace be upon him). I would pursue the Ghazis in their tracks, cook food for them and do dressing for the injured and make arrangements for treatment of the diseased. [Narrated by al-Bukhari in al-Sahih, 1:333 §937 & 2:595 §1569.]

This practice continued in the period of the rightly-guided Caliphs after the period of Prophethood. It is related in the books of sira that women were part of the parliament (majlis al-shura) during the period of 'Umar b. al-Khattab (may Allah be well pleased with him). [Narrated by 'Abd al-Razzaq in al-Musannaf, 6:180 §10420.] During the rule of 'Uthman (may Allah be well pleased with him), women were designated as ambassadors to other countries. [Related by al-Tabari in Tarikh al-Umam wa al-Muluk, 2:601.]

In a similar manner the history of Islam is replete with the mention of women who obtained distinguished positions in the fields of hadith sciences, the science of interpretation, jurisprudence, medical science, poetry and calligraphy. [Shaykh-ul-Islam Dr Muhammad Tahir-ul-Qadri, Women Rights in Islam.]

It is thus imperative, if a nation wishes to be successful and move towards a sustainable reality, the women of that society must be given every opportunity to attain knowledge and education which is not only her due but a right that has been ordained to her by Almighty Allah♡

CHAPTER SIX

Womens Role in Society

There are too many misconceptions about Muslim women. It is considered that women in Islam are oppressed or under the burden of men's scrutiny. This is generally a statement made by those who are the disbelievers of Allah. The true Muslims who know the reality of Qur'an are aware of the fact and the special status that has been given to women in Islam. Muslim women, be daughters, wives, or mothers are elevated in the eyes of society as well as Allah. In this blog article, we bring to you some Hadiths as quoted by Allah (S.W.T.) to spread the knowledge of Muslim women's role in society.

Islam raises the status of women and honors their minds and capabilities, but without making women like men. In Islam, like men, women are charged with religious duties.

Allah (S.W.T.) said:

> "*"Verily, the Muslim men and women who submit to Allah in Islam, the believers men and women who believe in Islamic Monotheism, the men and*

> *the women who are obedient to Allah, the men and women who re truthful in their speech and deeds, the men and women who are patient in performing all the duties that Allah has ordered and in abstaining from all that Allah has forbidden, the men and the women who are humble before Allah, the men and the women who give Sadaqat, the men and the women who observe fast in the month of Ramadan, the men and the women who guard their chastity from illegal sexual acts, and the men and the women who remember Allah much with their hearts and tongues. Allah has prepared for them forgiveness and a great rewards in the form of Paradise." (Qur'an 33:35)*"

Women in Islam have a strong stature. They are held accountable for their own actions and are not held responsible for the actions of their husbands and their fathers. So if a woman is righteous then she cannot be harmed by the wickedness of her husband. Conversely, if she is evil and does not have noble virtues then she does not have any share in the righteousness of her husband. Each is an individual responsible for his or her own actions..

Allah (S.W.T.) said:

> "*"Allah sets forth an example for those who disbelieve: the wife of the Nuh and the wife of the Lat. They were under two of our righteous slaves,*

> *but they both betrayed their husbands by rejecting their doctrine. So they availed their respective wives not against Allah, and it was said: 'Enter the fire along with those who enter!'. And Allah has set forth an example for those who believe, the wife of Fir'aun, when she said,: 'My Lord! Build for me a home with you in Paradise., and save me from Fir'aun and his work, and save me from the people who are polytheists, wrong-doers and disbelievers in Allah."*"

Thus, we see through the light of Islam and Qur'an that Muslim women displays a strong position in society and are elevated with their noble deeds towards their husband, children, family, and society as a whole.

CHAPTER SEVEN

True meaning of Pardah

In Islam, Pardah is referred to as the seclusion of women from men who are deemed as Na-Mahram for her. Pardah is fulfilled by observing a veil to hide herself from the sight of any Na-Mahram. Na-Mahrams are the ones with whom the women and the men are not allowed to be alone with like cousin brothers or sisters, uncles, aunt, etc.

How Muslims offend Pardah?

Pardah is treated as a very less important virtue especially by today's youth. In the sake of development, society has developed into a more open environment with a mixed gathering of both genders. Today, Muslim men and women who are compete strangers do not find any Haya in talking to each other and spending time along with one another. Such a behavior is not considered to be modest.

What happens when a man and a woman are along together?

Shaitaan takes great pleasure in keeping a Muslim man and woman who are not married to each other stay alone together. He tempts them to commit a sin so that the person is taken far away from Allah.

It is said in Qur'an,

> "*A man is never alone with a woman (i.e., a woman who is neither his wife nor a female relative that he is allowed to be alone with) except that the third one with them is shaitaan. (Sahihul-jami: 2546).*"

So, at any point of time when a Muslim man and woman who are Na-Mahram are alone with one another, Shaitaan accompanies them throughout and tempts them to sin further. A prolonged stare is probably the first preliminary step that result in fornication.

Advice in the light of Islam

Every noble and modest Muslim sister must take all necessary precautions to avoid personal meetings with a man. Not only strangers but any male cousin, or brother-in-law or uncle should not be allowed to spend alone time with you. For this you can take care that you limit your conversations with men. You should try to not shake hands while talking to men for any work related purpose. Also, you should restrict yourself from having eye contact as much as possible.

CHAPTER EIGHT

ribute to all Muslim womens

This topic is a tribute to all Muslim womens who sometimes feel less-worthy and under-estimate their value. This topic is a motivation motivation for women to lift up your spirits in case you have been facing some blues lately. Many of us are aware of the elevated status that has been set for Muslim women in Islam. But it is important to remember those Hadith from time to time so you can share and care.

As a daughter, opens the door Jannah...

The Prophet (P.B.U.H.) said;

> "*He, who has two daughters and takes care of them in a befitting manner, he and I will be in paradise as close as two fingers.*"

A daughter brings a whole atmosphere of positivity in the house. With her childish and caring nature, she never fails to make others happy. A home with daughters always echoes with unending laughter.

As a Wife, completes half of the Imaan of her husband.

Qur'an says,

> "
>
> *Greatest blessing after Imaan is a virtuous wife.*"

The wife is the most precious person for a man. She makes a home into a safe haven by her virtues. She not only becomes the shield for her husband but be her support through every thick and thin. As it is said that only good men deserve good women. It is because women have the power to make or break a home.

As a Mother, Jannah comes beneath her feet.

Qur'an says,
Jannah lies beneath the feet of the mother.

How lost is every child without a mother? A child might be closest to his father but no one can replace the position of her mother. She is a friend, a guide, a teacher, a philosopher. She sacrifices her whole life for the happiness of her children only to build a brighter future.

CHAPTER NINE

Women and Backbiting

Backbiting – "malicious rumour about someone who is not present". If a person backbites, on the contrary, he/she is eating his/her deceased brother's meat. Allah says in the Holy Quran in Surah Al- Hujrath 49 chapter about backbiting.

The women chatter and backbite more than men. The reason women follow Dajal than men is that of backbiting.

Woman's fulfilment is boundless. Possessiveness and envious nature is the trademark of women.

Since women are weaker than men. They constantly desire the sympathy of others. Though they have absolute patience. They are intellectual and daring, but their bodily appearance pulls them down.

Women and Duniya:

Women's classic styles are comparison and jealousy which is still prevailing among them. They prejudice others. The other factor of women is that if they detest or avoid someone, they prefer their relatives, acquaintances also to avoid, detest the same person.

For example, a cold war between mother-in-law and daughter-in-law. Because the mother might feel insecure and the wife will need her husband's support every time. The typical style of two women.

The next factor is bias or prestige in the property. Women are most keen on prestige and social affairs. They demand the posh life rather than a convenient life. Women of high status or accomplishments will scorn a woman proficient to her.

The women who have handsome sons will discourage every girl. They might have the attitude that their sons are the Mr Universe.

Likewise, if the wife has a smart husband, thus she might be saucy and selfish on the other women.

Gossip vs relationship:

Backbiting and gossip often destroy reputations and disunify relationships. If a person backbites or gossips about someone, the hearer will have negative assessments. It will affect the speaker too.

Few people might assume the speaker knows no other job else than slander., the hearer will spill the beans to others.

Further, it is always the best to never involve the third person in your relationship. Though it might be our parents.

If you share the hardships with your parents do in front of your spouse. So it does not result in gossip or backbite. For instance, a few parents might think their spouse is snappish. They might also think you are afraid of your spouse and talk about him/her in their absence.

When you are in dolour stage and if you share your obscurities do not weep. None of the parents will enjoy when their child weeps. For parents, their children are more precious than gems.

They might chastise, pester, shrew, and punish you. But they will not on any moment adore if another person flogs or abuses you. In specific, if you are the only child, daughter or son then you might be the apples of one's eye. Their clemency will break one day. On that day the parents might react as eggs are eggs. Unwanted miscommunication and vengeance will thrive in the hearts of the parents and the speaker.

The second stage of the gossip:

At the final stage, parents will not tolerate any more they will give some ideas to defend against your spouse or they will ask you to be patient. The communication between the spouse and parents will descend slowly.

Instead of getting dependent on your spouse, the ideas of your parents will make you bold and strong to raise your voice. A husband will raise his hand and a wife will abuse her husband through her tongue.

At this stage, you will become close to a person who favours your actions and turns against people who do not favour you.

Though they might be your relatives or friends.

Parents vengeance and their sympathy might also be the reason for your divorce. Because we all the followers of our parents especially after marriage we might become very close to our mother. We might follow her advice and step in each action we take.

So it is better at any moment not to include your parents in your relationship. You might very well know about your spouse than family members and friends.

It is parents psychology to show their concern towards children. They fix their mind with a tendency where the offsprings are still young. Especially mother's. She might still treat you as a toddler who falls in the new steps of life. The pampering of the mother never ends.

Last stage of backbiting:

This behaviour often shows a lack of respect, acceptance, compassion, loyalty, friendliness, justice, kindness, truthfulness, and unity in relationships.

The Holy Qur'an says, "Woe to the backbiter, even if his tale is true, for the taint is in his motive."

Try to avoid backbiting and gossip, which can happen when you discuss private details about someone or something with friends, family members.

As gossip moves from one person to the next, the information often becomes embellished, which may cause harm or embarrassment to you and spouse.

Try to share something positive about your spouse under negative discussion instead.

Just think, how will your spouse react when spoken about him/her whether he/she dislikes and become unhappy about what you said?

Communicate about the issues directly with your spouse than to speak about your spouse behind their backs.

Couples can talk about and agree on how they will communicate respectfully about each other when they are privately together.

The spouse often shares information about their relationships with mutual friends and family members. This includes topics such as marriages, divorces, pregnancies, and births.

Before sharing the information, just think whether it will strengthen your relationship or break. Always speak positively about your spouse. A single drop of water makes an ocean.

Never be unsatisfied of your spouse. Verily, Allah curses the partner who is unhappy and pester their spouse.

OMG, DID YOU HEAR ABOUT... HOW TO AVOID GOSSIPING?

So, as i am a female and we all know how easy it is to get sucked into the newest story of shabeena and how shabeena and that boy lack are no longer engaged. Or how shabeena is no longer employed by that big university. Or how shabeena and her Brother cum Buddy sharik are no longer Best friends. Although these things may just seem like "happenings", they really are the newest gossip. So for argument's sake, let me define exactly what "gossip" is. According to the Oxford English Dictionary, gossip is the idle talk about the affairs of others, whether they are good or bad. Yes, sisters- GOOD or BAD.

Ghibah (Gossip) is something that is very frowned upon in Islam.

As Prophet Muhammad (SAW) said,

> "
>
> *"A person may utter a word he thinks harmless, which results in his falling the depth of seventy years into hellfire."* "

I know resisting to gossip is hard. And I also know how abundant it is in our society today. BUT I can also tell you that there are several things you can do to avoid it all.

IT'S A SMALL WORLD

Always remember that whatever is circulating might just come back to the person it is about. Do you really want to have your name on that sin? Also realize that once you are a labeled gossip, you might not be seen as so trustworthy. Therefore, some of your closest friends might find it hard to come to you. Gossiping can lead to many things, including broken friendships and trust.

SILENCE IS GOLDEN

Secondly, try not to listen to the gossip. You know which of your friends is the 'social butterfly,' so try to engage in other conversations with her. If she somehow manages to bring up something about another person, remain silent. You do not have to answer in any way, unless it is to disprove her statement. Yes, it is wrong to be talking about another person, good or bad, but if you are doing it for the sake of helping them, then it is perfectly fine (just be sure you are positive about what you say.)

For example:

ABC girL Gossip: "Oh did you hear about shabeena? She's thinking about breaking up with that boy."

You: ".. Hmm, I was just talking to shabeena the other day and she said everything is fine.

DIP OUT

Thirdly, do no get caught up on gossipy conversations. For example- you are out with a group of girls at a restaurant and as you are waiting for the food to arrive, Soaad brings up something about Somaya which creates a huge topic of conversation. Simply excuse yourself and go to the restroom. This is the best way to eliminate yourself from the conversation and avoid temptation to respond.

"SPEAKING OF!.. WHAT DID YOU THINK OF THAT..."

Interrupting a gossip session with a different topic also seems to work very well. Say your friends are too busy talking about XYZ person and how he/she really wasn't playing that well during last week's game. Instead of continuing the banter about XYZ person, bring up something about another sport. Like: "Did you see that match on ABC Person's last night?" Hopefully, they would get the hint and stop talking about XYz.

There you have it, girls. There are many ways to avoid the ever growing problem of gossip- especially in the female world. If every person tries to withhold their judgments, I'm sure this world will be a much happier and better place insha'Allah.

***Remember, Prophet Muhammad (SAW) said: "The one who adheres to the lengthy silence (except from that which is good)* will be saved on the Day of Judgment.**

CHAPTER TEN

My Hijab My Protector

In Islam, women and men are required to dress modestly. Islam enjoins specifically on women to cover their head with a piece of clothing called veil or Hijab in the presence of men outside of the immediate family, also known as Mahram.

•*HIJAB– Most common type of headscarf that covers the head and neck. Hijab can be worn in different colors and styles.*

•*BURQA– Burqa covers everything and only eyes are visible through a mesh.*

•*NIQAB– Burqa and Niqab are almost similar. Niqab covers the full body and only eyes are visible.*

Hijab has always been a topic for debate, or sometimes, a discreetly avoided subject, seldom really talked about by the people around us. However, for the Muslim women

who practiced the custom of Hijab, it was never even a question. However, other women and young girls who wore Hijab without knowing their importance were often confused.
To understand its importance, one should know that modesty has been part and parcel of the Islamic culture all through. Hijab encourages modesty, both physically and spiritually. When a woman covers her head as per Allah's command, it is her way of showing her belief in Allah and accepting all his commands. It makes the connection between the Almighty and that woman stronger.

> "*"And tell the believing women to reduce of their vision and guard their private parts and not expose their adornment except that which appears thereof and to wrap their headcovers over their chests and not expose their adornment except to their husbands, fathers, sons, husband's sons, brothers, brother's son, sister's sons..." [Qur'an 24:31]*"

This verse in the Holy Quran tells us that Hijab is a religious obligation, and every woman faithful to Islam should cover their head. A woman who wears a hijab doesn't show off her beauty. Allah protects a woman who covers her head at all times as Hijab acts as the Almighty's shield from all the sinful gazes. It allows men and women to communicate correctly, eliminating lustful/dirty thoughts. By removing their veil, they would be removing Allah's protection against evil.

For many women, wearing Hijab is a confidence booster in itself. It's about taking pride in Islam. There is a lot of wisdom in wearing Hijab, which makes these women who cover their heads extraordinary. Apart from this, it also brings obedience to one's face. I've always been fascinated by the kind of glow a woman, who wears a hijab, has! Women who cover their heads should know about its importance very well to answer questions ever asked about it.

However, Islam is a very understanding religion. There is relaxation in following Islamic norms in an emergency like visiting a doctor, filing a complaint, etc.

Bottom Line

Veil/Hijab is an integral part of Islam. Women practice wearing Hijab as it is Allah's command to his believers. Apart from this, there are several different reasons to like veils, as it is a sign of obedience, chastity, and purity. It is Allah's way of testing his people!

CHAPTER ELEVEN

Before You say QabooL Hai

Taking a step towards Nikah is one of the most important steps of anyone's life. We all feel different kinds of pressures like emotional, social, and even financial before entering the knots of matrimony. As much as people talk about life and etiquettes Muslim should observe after his/her Nikah, we also need to discuss more what we need to do before way finally say yes. Qubool Hai is just two words that are powerful enough to change one's life forever.We have some simple guidelines for you that will help you to think thoroughly before you make any final move. Firstly, you should introspect yourself to know the reason why you need a partner. Nikah is a lifetime commitment. So, it is very important to talk to oneself because you are looking for a person with whom you will build your family.

Next, while you are looking for a spouse, you need to talk more. Even if you are introvert it becomes your responsibility to take care of what is being discussed about your future. Nobody knows you better than yourself. You should communicate with your parents and elders about what you need in your spouse. Communication is the key to making the final choice.

When you are finding the right person for Nikah, it does not mean that you can take the chance of looking at the person or talk to him/her in a flirtatious manner. If you decide your potential spouse before making the decision, make sure that you lower your gaze.

> "
>
> *Tell the believing men to lower their gaze and be modest. That is purer for them. Lo! Allah is aware of what they do" (Quran 24:30).*
> *"And tell the believing women to lower their gaze and be modest, and to display of their adornment only that which is apparent, and to draw their veils over their bosoms..." (Quran 24:31).* "

Always remember to involve your parents or guardians to meet under their scrutiny. Meeting alone is not a very wise decision.

> "*The Prophet said: "Whenever a man is alone with a woman the Shaytan makes a third"* "

So, before you go to meet the person clear your head with what you are expecting from a life partner and what questions you need to ask.

What questions to ask your potential spouse?

If you are thinking to step into the process of finding your spouse, we are sure your heart and mind must be undergoing a brainstorming session of infinite questions. Considering someone for Nikah brings with it a list of questions that you need to ask to know about that person and family. Family background cannot say much about the nitty-gritty of the person's nature, aspirations, habits, and Deen. This requires that the Muslim families who are involved in the Nikah of their children should allow them to interact under their guidance.

Why do you think such interaction is necessary?

You will be surprised to know but most of the marriages break because of the misunderstandings and mismatch of personalities. If the bride and groom can interact and discuss what is necessary before their Nikah, it can save a lot of Halal relationships and homes...

Confused about what questions to ask? Let me help you.

Questions about Deen.

> ***"How often do you recite Qur'an?***
>
> ***Do you pray regularly and observe fasting?***
>
> ***Do you prefer going to Islamic classes or listen to Islamic lectures?***
>
> ***What are your plans regarding Hajj and Umrah for the future?***
>
> ***How much you try to follow the Sunnah of Prophet as stated in Qur'an in your lifestyle?"***

Questions about Education.

"What are your qualifications? what motivated you to study this far?

Do you plan to pursue your studies after Nikah?

Do you wish to complete your studies and then marry?

How much time will you take to complete your studies?

Do you want to have a career in the same education field?

Questions about Career and dreams.

What is our biggest dream? Do you have any plans for the same?

Are you currently working?

Does your workplace allow you to practice Islam?

Do you wish to work after Nikah? If not, do you wish to start your own business?

Will you be okay if you are not allowed to work in a company after Nikah? (especially to be asked from Muslim women)"

Question about Family.

"Which family structure do you prefer? Nuclear or joint family?

How many siblings do you have and their whereabouts?

How is your relationship with your father and mother?

What do they expect from you in terms of Nikah?

What is the background of your father and mother?"

Questions about personality.

"*What are your habits? Your favourite hobbies?*

How emotionally expressive are you?

Would you like to take care of my parents after nikah?

Do you like to cook? Do you prefer any particulate?

Do you have habits like smoking?

What kind o movies and places do you prefer?

How big is our friend circle? Who are your close friends?"

Questions about expectations.

"*What kind of a spouse are you looking for in terms of qualities and personality traits?*

Do you expect to become a mother soon?

What are your opinions about husband and wife roles in the family?

How would you want to share the responsibilities at home?

How do you think Nikah will help us to elevate our Deen?"

These are some of the potential questions that you can mask from the person you are considering for Nikah. Such interactions are very important as they play a crucial role in our Nikah decision. love to know about your ideas.

CHAPTER TWELVE

Misconceptions About Women

Men and women were created by Allah (SWT) without being subjected to one another.
Islam has ensured gender equality and women's rights in every aspect of their lives.
Islam ensures that men and women have equal rights and that there is no discrimination between them.

Can women recite Quran during periods?

Yes, a woman can recite the Quran during her periods.
Women used to menstruate during the time of Allah's Messenger, and if reciting was haram for them, as it is for men, then this would have been one of the things that the Prophet [SAW] forbade to his ummah, and the Mothers of the Believers would have known about it and passed it onto the people.
However, it is not permissible for the woman to touch the Holy Quran without gloves, a handkerchief, or a clean piece of cloth. It is permissible for her to recite without touching it.

Therefore, It is not permissible to make it haram.

Can women offer Namaz during periods?

It is haram for a menstrual woman to pray both Farz and nafil prayers, and if she does, the prayers are not valid. In Islam, there is a saying that "difficulty brings ease," which means that when a person is going through a difficult time, Islam will make certain concessions to make life easier.

So the issue isn't that women are "not allowed" to pray, but instead that they are exempted from doing so because these responsibilities are arduous and time-consuming.

Can women fast during periods?

No, a woman should not fast during her periods. In fact, it is haram to do so.

Allah has forbidden menstrual women from fasting out of pity for them because blood loss weakens them, and if a woman fasted while menstruating, she would be weakened both by menstruation and by fasting, making it an unjust burden and possibly hazardous.

If a woman has her period while fasting, her fast is nullified, even if it occurs shortly before Maghrib, and she must make up that day if it was an obligatory fast.

However, she has to make up for all the missed fasts once her periods are over.

Can women pray Taraweeh in Mosque?

A female praying Tarawih or other prayers in the Mosque is perfectly acceptable. The basic principle for a woman's prayer is that she should pray at home. Still, suppose she believes there is an interest to be served by praying in a mosque, as long as she covers herself adequately, because it is more motivating for her or because she can benefit from listening to lessons. In that case, there is nothing wrong with that.

It's also beneficial because it has numerous benefits and encourages individuals to do nice things.

If a woman is afraid of being lethargic at home, the Mosque is preferable. However, if that is necessary, there is nothing wrong with it.

CHAPTER THIRTEEN

Keeping Connection With God during Menstruation

It is often difficult for a Muslim woman to understand why she is unable to make salah (ritual prayer) for five days or so. Many may feel that it is a limitation on them due to their gender. Others may misunderstand this, and think that they can not engage in any Islamic activities through the duration of their menses.

This is simply not so. Many women suffer from extreme cramps, heavy bleeding, nausea, headaches, and other maladies during their cycle. It is truly a sign of the mercy of Allah Almighty that we are excused from prayer during this time. I know more than one sister who would be unable to perform the physical duties of the prayer during her cycle.

In a hadith narrated Abu Sa'id Al-Khudri and Abu Huraira the Prophet said:

"

"No fatigue, nor disease, nor sorrow, nor sadness, nor hurt, nor distress befalls a Muslim, even if it were the prick he receives from a thorn, but that Allah expiates some of his sins for that." (Reported by Al-Bukhari.)"

When a Muslim woman reads this hadith she aught to be satisfied that Allah Almighty was not unjust with her, simply because she knows that through the days of menstruation she is to be rewarded for her patience on the fatigue she is experiencing. She will be rewarded as if she had done all her creedal duties without any loss.

On the other hand, Islam does not ask the Muslim woman to give up her spiritualities or pursuit of Islamic knowledge during this time either. While it is true that she cannot perform ritual prayers, Tawaf (circumambulation of the Ka`bah) and fasting; however, she is not prohibited from listening to tapes of the Qur'an, or from listening to someone else recite it. She may even recite the verses to herself silently. She can still pray, through du`aa' (supplication), and can still repeat the praises of Allah Almighty (perform dhikr during this time as well. There is also nothing to stop her from reading Islamic texts outside of the Qur'an, including hadith.

A Menstruating wife in Islam

Islam is guided with a set of morals and manners even for the actions of intimacy between a husband and a wife. Marital relations are the most pious relations between a man and a woman on this Earth, intimacy with your

menstruating wife has some regulations that you must be aware of.
It is not permissible to perform intercourse with a menstruating woman.

> “
>
> ***Allah says,***
>
> ***“They ask you concerning intercourse during menstruation. Say, It is harmful to both the partners so keep away from women during menses and do not approach them until they are clean. When they h have purified themselves, approach them from where Allah permitted you. Indeed, Allah loves those who constantly repent and loves those who purify themselves.” [Al-Baqarah 2:222]***”

However, the Muslim man should not be confused as he is permissible to sleep next to his menstruating wife, touch her, caress her, and so on. Treat them like the normal days except the action of intercourse.

> “*Allah says,*
>
> *“They ask you concerning intercourse during menstruation. Say, It is harmful to both the partners so keep away from women during menses and do not approach them until they are clean. When they h have purified themselves, approach them from where Allah permitted you. Indeed, Allah loves those who constantly repent and loves those who purify themselves.” [Al-Baqarah 2:222]*”

However, the Muslim man should not be confused as he is permissible to sleep next to his menstruating wife, touch her, caress her, and so on. Treat them like the normal days except the action of intercourse.

The Prophet (Peace be Upon Him) said,

"Live with them in the house, and do anything you wish except for intercourse."

It is very important to spread awareness as it is crucial for the health of both spouses. Some people are unaware and hence go on to fulfil their pleasures. However, as good and noble Muslims you should strive to observe the guidelines that have been stated in Qur'an and followed by the Prophet (Peace Be Upon Him).

"When the Prophet (P.B.U.H.) wanted to have intimacy with one oh his wives while she was menstruating, he would have wrap a piece of cloth around her lower body and would then fondle her." [al-Bukhari]

"When the Prophet (P.B.U.H.) wanted something intimate from a menstruating wife, he would first cover her private area with a piece of cloth." [al-Albani]

After a woman's menses ends, it is recommended for her to perform ghusl before her husband try to be intimate with her because this is the highest form of purification. She should cleanse her body as soon as the cycle ends.

CHAPTER FOURTEEN

How important is Compatibility in Nikah

Compatibility between two partners is still given less priority to other factors like beauty and wealth. However, compatibility reflects the balancing factor between a couple and makes the obligations in Nikah more simpler. When Nikah is performed between two people who have the right balance of compatibility, then there are greater chances of a happier life. In many cases where the partners turned to the unfortunate decision of separation, it was mainly because they were incompatible for one another which made life more difficult. A man should seek a wife who is compatible with him and a woman should seek a husband who is compatible with her.

Aishah R.A. reported that Allah's Messenger, the Prophet (Peace be upon him) said,

"Make good choice for your seed: marry women who are compatible to you, and marry your daughters to them who are compatible."

[Recorded by Ibn Majah, al-Hakim, and others]

What is the definition of compatibility in Islam?

In Islam, compatibility comprises of two major dimensions: *Deen and Character*. These two virtues are such that they cannot be compromised and become the focal point for compatibility. A man or woman who is lacking in either of them is a poor candidate and should not be considered if you want to have a happier Nikah.

Other qualities might also add to the compatibility between the two spouses but they would not be mandatory except these two. Other important factors that enhance compatibility are age, language, financial status, family status, national background, education, etc. With an understanding of all different factors, the decision for choosing the spouse should be carefully taken.

However, one must understand that except for Deen and Character, all of the other qualities are of secondary nature and should not be necessarily overplayed. Especially, they should not be used as grounds for discrimination based on race, social status, wealth, country of origin, etc.

So, it is advisable to seek advice from your friends and elders and try to make a wise choice. Compatibility leads to better relationships and makes happier and healthier homes.

CHAPTER FIFTEEN

What are your rights upon your Husband?

A Muslim woman is bestowed upon numerous rights upon her Husband. After the Nikah, the Muslim man becomes the sole protector, bread earner, and pleasure giver for his wife. In return, the woman leaves her home, family, and friends only to start a new life with his husband. Meanwhile all this, some men tend to become very controlling and try to exercise unjustified power over their wives. In this male-dominated world, women should not feel weak and should not forget the rights that are made specially to protect them. Today we will be discussing the different rights that make the married life of Muslim women simpler and easier. Awareness is the key to knowledge. So without any further delay let us look at those rights.

Qur'an says,

O mankind, fear your Lord, who created you from one soul and created from its mate and dispersed from both of them many men and women. And fear Allah, through whom you ask one another, and the wombs. Indeed Allah is ever, over you, an Observer. (Qur'an 4:1)

• *In no case should a woman find it okay that his husband has the right to harm her physically, mentally, or emotionally.*

• *You will find happiness with a man whose heart beats with softness for you and prays for your Aakhirah. The man who has hidden objectives with you do not deserve your respect.*

• *A man should only marry a woman if he is ready to take the full responsibility of a woman. In case the husband is ignorant and does not contribute towards his responsibilities, then the woman has the right to raise her voice against the injustice.*

• *Marital relations should not be aimed for a single-side pleasure. The sole purpose should not be the extension of the family. But it should involve cuddling and lovely playfulness so as to make the wife feel special.*

• *The husband must try to keep the love growing taking the mutual responsibility of making a healthy relationship.*

• *The best trait to look in a wife is her Imaan. Inner beauty should always the priority of every man instead of outer beauty. So, a man has no right to insult his wife on her appearance publicly or personally*

• *The husband should make the household chores rigid to gender roles. Instead, he should be more cooperative in helping her wife do all the work.*

• *The husband should protect the chastity of his wife and must ensure that she is not looked upon by any evil eye.*

So, these were some of the rights of Muslim wives over their husbands as talked about in Qur'an. What according to you are other rights that Muslim women should be more aware of ♡

احترم المرأة

LEARN PATIENCE FROM ASIYAH r.a

LOYALTY FROM KHADIJAH r.a

PURITY FROM MARYAM r.a

SINCERITY FROM A'ISHAH r.a

STEADFASTNESS FROM FATIMAH r.a

So

Never Disrespect A Women when Allah (swt) dedicated A whole surah called surah An-Nisa...

9 798889 758389

Printed by Libri Plureos GmbH in Hamburg,
Germany